MW00560450

Also from Linda Roberts

A Companion to *The Chronological Bible Workbook*

- Answers

- Completed Charts

- Links to Full Color Maps and Photos

- Additional Information

- Academic & Calendar Year Teaching Schedules

The Answer Key

The Answer Key is the teaching tool for *The Chronological Bible Workbook*. It provides a way to check the accuracy of all answers when using *The Chronological Bible Workbook* as a personal study or in a small group, home school, or traditional Bible class setting. Additional information has also been provided to assist in stimulating class discussion.

The Answer Key can be purchased from Amazon, Barnes and Noble, and WestBow Press online bookstores.

The Chronological Bible Workbook

A STUDY GUIDE AS EVENTS OCCURRED IN TIME

Linda J. Roberts

WESTBOW
PRESS®
A DIVISION OF THOMAS NELSON
& ZONDERVAN

Copyright © 2016 Linda J. Roberts.

All rights reserved. No part of this book may be used or reproduced by any means, graphic, electronic, or mechanical, including photocopying, recording, taping or by any information storage retrieval system without the written permission of the author except in the case of brief quotations embodied in critical articles and reviews.

Scriptures taken from the Holy Bible, New International Version®, NIV®. Copyright © 1973, 1978, 1984, 2011 by Biblica, Inc.™ Used by permission of Zondervan. All rights reserved worldwide. www.zondervan.com The "NIV" and "New International Version" are trademarks registered in the United States Patent and Trademark Office by Biblica, Inc.™

This book is a work of non-fiction. Unless otherwise noted, the author and the publisher make no explicit guarantees as to the accuracy of the information contained in this book and in some cases, names of people and places have been altered to protect their privacy.

WestBow Press books may be ordered through booksellers or by contacting:

WestBow Press
A Division of Thomas Nelson & Zondervan
1663 Liberty Drive
Bloomington, IN 47403
www.westbowpress.com
1 (866) 928-1240

Because of the dynamic nature of the Internet, any web addresses or links contained in this book may have changed since publication and may no longer be valid. The views expressed in this work are solely those of the author and do not necessarily reflect the views of the publisher, and the publisher hereby disclaims any responsibility for them.

Any people depicted in stock imagery provided by Thinkstock are models, and such images are being used for illustrative purposes only.
Certain stock imagery © Thinkstock.

ISBN: 978-1-5127-4570-2 (sc)
ISBN: 978-1-5127-4569-6 (e)

Library of Congress Control Number: 2016909871

Print information available on the last page.

WestBow Press rev. date: 10/15/2019

Dedication

This workbook is dedicated to God who purposed and prepared me; to my parents who taught me about God; to my mom who instilled a passion for books; to my "Jonathan" who helped me plot, plan, and persevere; and to the members of the ladies' class at the church of Christ in Rolla, Missouri, who accompanied me on this journey through God's Word from beginning to end. All have provided insight, inspiration, and encouragement. What a trip!

"Your Word is a lamp to my feet and a light for my path" (Psalm 119:105).

Special Dedication

My younger brother, Steven, was a man of great faith and abiding love. He loved God, His Son, Jesus, and the Holy Spirit. He loved the Word of God. He loved his earthly and spiritual families. He loved the lost. Cancer took his life in January 2014. After receiving a terminal diagnosis, Steve vowed to continue to glorify God with his life so others would be drawn to Him. Like my brother, I also strive to glorify God so others will want to know Him. In all I do, I honor You.

We are not human beings having a temporary spiritual experience. We are spiritual beings having a temporary human experience.

—Pierre Teilhard de Chardin

Contents

Preface xiii

Introduction xv

In the Beginning 1
(Creation–2100 BC)

    Creation: The Beginning of All Things 1

    Adam and Eve: The Beginning of the Human Race...2

    Noah..3

    The Tower of Babel: The Beginning of All Nations 4

The Patriarchs 6
(2100–1525 BC)

    Abram: The Beginning of God's Covenant with the Israelites 6

        Lot..7

        Covenant Established between God and Abram..7

        Name Changes 8

        Sodom and Gomorrah 8

    Isaac..9

    Jacob and Esau 11

    Joseph..14

A Nation Set Free 18
(1525–1400 BC)

    Moses and the Israelites in Egypt 18

    The Plagues..19

    The Passover and the Exodus 20

    Covenant Established between God and Israel...23

        Covenant Broken 25

        Covenant Renewed 25

    The Building of the Tabernacle and the Beginning of Temple Worship.......26

    The Establishment of Priests and Instructions for Temple Worship...........26

    The Establishment of New Laws...27

    The Journey through the Desert...28

    Joshua, Israel's New Leader 32

    Moses's Review of Israelite History...33

The Laws of Moses...35
(1450–1400 BC)

    Religious Laws 35
    Laws of Government..37
    Judicial Laws 37
    Criminal Laws 38
    Civil Laws and Laws Governing Personal Behavior........................39
    Laws Governing Health and the General Welfare............................40
    Laws Governing Warfare 40
    Personal Responsibilities within These Laws 41

The Israelites' Arrival in Canaan: The Beginning of Life in the
Promised Land.. 42
(1400–1100 BC)

    The Renewal of the Covenant between God and Israel.................... 42
    Joshua's Leadership 42
    Moses's Death 43
    The Conquest of Canaan 43
    Joshua's Death..46
    The Period of the Judges 47
    The Story of Ruth 53
    Samson.. 54

The Kings of Israel..57
(1100–930 BC)

    Samuel as God's Servant 57
    King Saul 61
    David and His Psalms 62
    King David 68
    Psalms...75
        For a Troubled Soul 75
        Righteousness vs. Wickedness...76
        Joy and Praise 76
        Various Themes..76
        Messianic 77
    King Solomon 77
        Solomon's Proverbs...83
        Solomon's Song of Songs..93
        Solomon's Ecclesiastes..93
        Solomon's Death 95

Israel Divided 96
(930–725 BC)

Israel and Judah 96

Prophets and Prophecies 101

    Elijah 101

    Ahab and Jezebel 102

    Elisha 104

    Obadiah 106

    Joel 109

    Jonah 111

    Hosea 112

    Amos 113

    Isaiah 115

    Micah 116

Captivity Begins 117

Syria, Israel, and Judah at War 118

More Prophecies from Isaiah 118

    Regarding a Messiah 118

    Against Unfriendly Nations 119

    Regarding the Last Days 120

Israel Falls 121

Judah after the Fall of Israel 122
(725–585 BC)

More Prophecies from Isaiah 122

The End of Hezekiah's Reign 122

More Restoration and Messianic Prophecies from Isaiah 124

Nahum's Prophecies and King Josiah 126

Zephaniah's Prophecies 127

Josiah's Reforms 128

Jeremiah's Prophecies 128

Fall of Assyria and Rise of Babylon 131

Habakkuk 133

The First Judeans Exiled 133

Daniel and King Nebuchadnezzar 135

The Great Exile 136

Zedekiah as King 137

More Prophecies from Jeremiah 137

Ezekiel Prophesies from Exile 139

The Siege of Jerusalem 142

Prophecies from Jeremiah about a Spiritual Restoration 143

Ezekiel's Siege Prophecies from Babylon 144

Jeremiah's Death Threat in Jerusalem 145

Jerusalem Falls 146

Lamentations 146

A Remnant Escapes to Egypt 147

The Israelite Nation in Exile 149
(585–535 BC)

Ezekiel Prophesies about a Restoration 149

Shadrach, Meshach, and Abednego 150

Ezekiel's Temple Vision and His Death 151

Nebuchadnezzar's Insanity 152

The Story of Job 153

Exile Psalms 156

Daniel's Visions 157

Daniel in the Lions' Den 159

Restoration: Another New Beginning 160
(535–425 BC)

The Return to Jerusalem 160

Daniel's Final Vision 161

Problems with Temple Construction 161

Prophecies of Haggai and Zechariah 162

Temple Construction Completed 165

Psalms of a Restored Nation 165

More Prophecies from Zechariah 166

The Story of Esther 166

Malachi's Prophecies 169

Ezra and the Second Group of Exiles 170

Nehemiah 171

    The Rebuilding of the Wall around Jerusalem 171

    The Redistribution of the Population 172

    The Reform of Religious Practices 173

Israel's Official Records 174

The Time between the Testaments 175
(425–5 BC)

At the End of the Old Testament 175

The Apocryphal Writings 176

The Jews and the Greeks 176

The Jews and the Romans 177

A New Covenant through Christ: The Beginning of the Gospel Message 178
(5 BC–30 AD)

The Birth of Jesus and John the Baptist...178
Jesus's Flight to Egypt 181
The Early Years of Jesus...181
John the Baptist's Ministry 182
Satan's Temptation of Jesus 183
Jesus's Early Ministry...184
Jesus's Great Ministry in Galilee..186
Jesus's Sermon on the Mount 188
The Parables of Jesus 190
Jesus's Miracles 194
Apostles Are Sent Out 195
Jesus and the Multitudes 196
Preparing the Apostles for the End 199
Return to Jerusalem for Feast of Tabernacles..201
Jesus's Ministry from Galilee to Judea 203
Back in Jerusalem for Feast of Dedication.. 204
Jesus's Ministry in Perea.. 205
Jesus Raises Lazarus from the Dead 206
Jesus's Final Journey.. 208
    Triumphant Entry into Jerusalem 210
    The Last Supper...215
    Final Teachings to His Disciples...217
    Jesus's Betrayal and Arrest 218
    Jesus's Trial before the Sanhedrin 219
    Jesus's Trial before Pilate.. 220
    Jesus's Crucifixion 221
    Jesus's Burial... 222
    Jesus's Resurrection 223
    Jesus's Final Instructions and His Ascension 225

The Establishment of a New Body of Believers: The Beginning of Christianity 226
(30–100 AD)

Acts of Christ's Apostles.. 226
Stephen's Martyrdom 229
Persecution as the Gospel Is Spread... 230
Saul's Conversion 231
First Gentile Followers...232
More Persecution 234

Paul's Journeys and Letters 236
(46–67 AD)

    Paul's First Missionary Journey 236
    The Jerusalem Conference 238
    Paul's Letter to the Galatians 239
    Paul's Second Missionary Journey 241
    Paul's First Letter to the Thessalonians 244
    Paul's Second Letter to the Thessalonians 245
    Paul's Third Missionary Journey 246
    Paul's First Letter to the Corinthians 247
    Paul's Second Letter to the Corinthians 252
    Paul's Letter to the Romans 256
    Paul's Arrest and Trial before the Sanhedrin 262
    Paul before Governor Felix, Governor Festus, and King Agrippa 264
    Paul's Voyage to Rome 265
    Paul Under House Arrest in Rome 267
    Paul's Letter to the Colossians 268
    Paul's Letter to Philemon 270
    Paul's Letter to the Ephesians 271
    Paul's Letter to the Philippians 274
    Paul's First Letter to Timothy 276
    Paul's Letter to Titus 279
    Paul's Second Letter to Timothy 280

Additional Letters Written to Spread the Gospel Message 283
(50–95 AD)

    James's Letter 283
    Jude's Letter 286
    Peter's First Letter 287
    Peter's Second Letter 290
    The Letter to the Hebrews 292
    John's First Letter 297
    John's Second Letter 300
    John's Third Letter 300

The End of the Journey 301
(95–96 AD)

    The Revelation to John 301

Academic Year Study Schedule (36 weeks) 319
Calendar Year Study Schedule (52 weeks) 321
Bibliography 323
About the Author 325

Preface

On January 11, 2006, I began to teach F. LaGard Smith's *The Daily Bible In Chronological Order*, New International Version, Harvest House, 1984, to a Wednesday night ladies' Bible class. As I prepared my class notes each week, it struck me how often the Bible is taught topically, jumping from basic Bible stories to the life of Jesus to instruction on Christian principles. My degree in education, background in curriculum development, and teaching experience told me no instructor approaches a textbook in this manner. In school, class starts at the beginning of the textbook to provide information that will establish a strong foundation of basic concepts and finishes at the end where facts and ideas come together to provide a deeper understanding of the material.

The Bible is the greatest book ever written. This workbook treats the greatest book ever written like a textbook and is designed as a study tool for those who desire to look into God's Word starting at the beginning with Genesis and ending with the Revelation to John. This workbook is by no means exhaustive since one can spend a lifetime going deeper and deeper into God's Word; however, I believe a study that starts at the creation story and finishes with a look into the end times will allow God to reveal His Word in a way like no other.

Introduction

This workbook is designed to lead you on a journey through God's Word as events occurred in time. Your trip begins at God's creation of the world and ends with His revelation to John. Travel with God as He creates the world and establishes His relationship with all people. Experience the ups and downs of His relationship with the Israelite nation, culminating in her division, fall, and exile. See how God restores Israel and extends His covenant to all people through the birth, death, and resurrection of His Son, Jesus. Learn how early Christians and Christ's apostles were persecuted, but still successfully spread the gospel message. Travel with Paul on his missionary journeys, and study his letters to churches and individuals exhorting and encouraging them to keep the faith. Share in the messages of other letters written by James, Jude, Peter, the Hebrew writer and John. Finish your journey with God's revelation about Christ's return, and discover what will happen when time comes to an end. From the creation to Christ's second coming, this study will allow God to reveal His Word to your open heart and mind in a way like no other.

In the Beginning

(Creation–2100 BC)

> In this section, be prepared to discuss why God created the human race. Look for ways God used flawed people to carry out His divine purpose. Identify examples of how God blessed the faithful. Be able to give examples of humanity's deceit and describe the consequences of these sinful choices.

CREATION: THE BEGINNING OF ALL THINGS
Genesis 1:1–2:4

(Make the room as "cave" dark as possible. Use a penlight to read Genesis 1:1–2. At verse 3, turn on the light and continue reading through verse 5.)

What did the light separate?

What did the expanse/sky separate?

What did God create on day three?

> *Something to think about: What is the significance of seeds being created?*

What did God create on day four?

What was created on day five?

What was created on day six?

Who was created on day six?

> *Something to think about: How are human beings different from all other created creatures? How are all people created in "our image"? Who is the "our" mentioned in these verses?*

What did God do on the seventh day?

Why did God make this day holy?

ADAM AND EVE:
THE BEGINNING OF THE HUMAN RACE
Genesis 2:4–5:32

(Go to https://theologue.wordpress.com/2014/04/30/zaine-ridling-bible-atlas-e-book/. Look at Map 1, "The Ancient Near East.")

What was the garden called?

(Look at the map of "The Ancient Near East" and see if you can pinpoint where this garden might have been located.)

What one rule did God give to Adam?
What was the penalty if this rule was broken?
Who was created as a helper for Adam?
Explain how this was accomplished.
What tempted the woman?
What did the woman do after eating the fruit?
What was the result for Adam and the woman?

Something to think about: They broke the one rule, but did not die—or did they?

Explain what was produced as a result of their sin.

What was the woman named?
Why were the man and woman banished from the garden?

Who were the first two sons born to this couple?
Why was one son's offering not acceptable to God?
What did this son's anger cause him to do?

Discuss some of the consequences of anger.

Who was born to replace the son who was killed?
What type of men descended from Cain?
What type of men descended from Seth?
List the descendants from Adam to Noah. Include how long each man lived.

Something to think about: Why did men live so long at this time?

NOAH
Genesis 6:1–9:29

> *After you read this section, you should be able to give examples of Noah's great faith in God.*

What underlying factors contributed to humanity's moral decline?

How did the choices being made by the human race affect God?
Why did God send the flood?

Who found favor in God's eyes during this terrible time?
How did God plan to save this man and his family from the flood?

Why was this request such an act of faith?

> *Something to think about: Try to put yourself in Noah's shoes. Would you have had the faith of Noah?*

What was to go into the ark?

> *Something to think about: Why were more clean animals necessary?*

How old was Noah when the flood started?
How long did the deep springs and rains pour out water?

How long were the waters over the earth?
What caused the waters to recede?
Where did the ark finally settle?
How long did it take before the mountaintops were visible?
When did Noah send out the raven?
When did Noah send out the dove?
What happened to the dove?
When did Noah send the dove out again?
What was different when the dove returned this time?

When did Noah send out the dove again?
What happened to the dove this time?

How many days did it take for the earth to become completely dry?
What was the first thing Noah did after God called him out of the ark?
What covenant did God make with Noah?
What sign has God given for this covenant?
What caused Ham's descendants to be cursed?

What nation descended from Ham?
How old was Noah when he died?

THE TOWER OF BABEL:
THE BEGINNING OF ALL NATIONS
Genesis 10: 1 – 11: 32

(Go to https://theologue.wordpress.com/2014/04/30/zaine-ridling-bible-atlas-e-book/. Look at
Map 16, "The Table of Nations.")

What caused the creation of many languages and the scattering of the human race?

(Look at "The Table of Nations.")

Where did Noah's sons settle after the flood? What nations descended from each son?

List the descendants from Shem to Abram. Include how long each man lived.

Look back at the list of descendants from Adam to Noah.
Compare ages at birth of offspring and ages at which each man died.

What observations can you make? Think about how long Adam lived.

How old was Adam when Methuselah was born?
How old was Methuselah when Shem was born?
How many years between Adam and Abram?
Where was Abram born?

(Look back at the map of "The Ancient Near East." Find Abram's birthplace.)

Where was Terah headed when he settled the family in Haran?
Why did Terah take Abram and Sarai on this journey?

(Look at the map again. Locate Haran and Canaan.)

Why did Terah take the route he did?

Why did Lot go with Terah and his family?

Which wife was barren?
Why was this fact significant?

The Patriarchs

(2100–1525 BC)

> *After reading this section, you should be able to describe the covenant God established with His chosen people. You should also be able to give examples of how God used flawed individuals to accomplish His perfect plan.*

ABRAM: THE BEGINNING OF GOD'S COVENANT WITH THE ISRAELITES
Genesis 12:1–20

What did God ask Abram to do?

> *Something to think about: Put yourself in Abram's shoes. Would you have had the faith of Abram?*

What promises did God make to Abram?

(Go to https://theologue.wordpress.com/2014/04/30/zaine-ridling-bible-atlas-e-book/. Look at Map 18a, "The Land of Canaan Abraham to Moses," and Map 21a, "Abraham and Isaac and Jacob," and Map 21, "Abraham in Canaan.")

What land did God promise to Abram?
Why did Abram travel to Egypt?

(Look at the map of "Abraham in Canaan." Trace Abram's trip to Egypt and back.)

What deception did Abram plan?

Why do you think Abram felt he needed to have this plan?

How did the pharaoh treat Sarai? Why?

How did the pharaoh treat Abram?
What happened to change the pharaoh's attitude?

Lot
Genesis 13:1–14:20

Once back in Canaan, why did Abram and Lot go their separate ways?

(Look at the map of "Abraham in Canaan" again.)

What land did Lot choose?
What land did Abram choose?
What happened to Lot and his family after the battle in the Valley of Siddim?

What was Abram's response to the news?

After Abram's victory over Kedorloamer and the other kings, what did the king of Sodom want?

What was Abram's response?

Who was Melchizedek?
What did Abram give Melchizedek?

Covenant Established between God and Abram
Genesis 15:1–16:6

After reading this section, you should be able to describe how God used Abram to accomplish His plan. You should also be able to describe Abram's character, which allowed him to be used by God.

Why did Abram show concern about having an heir?
What was the Lord's response?

What was the significance of Abram's dream?

(Look back at the maps of "Abraham in Canaan," "Abraham, Isaac and Jacob," and "The Land of Canaan," and identify the land God promised to Abram.)

What suggestion did Sarai make to ensure Abram would have an heir?

Something to think about: What were the long-term consequences of Sarai's impatience?

When Hagar became pregnant, how did Sarai respond?
What promises did the angel of the Lord make to Hagar?

How old was Abram when Ishmael was born?

Name Changes
Genesis 17:1–18:15

How old was Abram when the Lord changed his name?
What was Abram's new name?
What action was required as a sign of God's covenant?

What was Sarai's new name?
How did Abraham respond when God repeated his promise that Sarah would be blessed by the birth of a son?

What name did God choose for this future son?
What message did the three heavenly visitors have?

What was Sarah thinking when she heard this?

How did the Lord respond?

Sodom and Gomorrah
Genesis 18:16–20:18

What did the three heavenly visitors tell Abraham before they left?

What bargain did Abraham make with the Lord?
When the two angels who had been with the Lord reached Sodom, what happened to them?

When they came to Lot's house, what did the Sodomite men want?

What did Lot offer instead?

What happened to the Sodomite men?

Why had the two angels been sent to Sodom and Gomorrah?

Who did the angels convince to flee?

What warning did the angels give?

What happened to Sodom and Gomorrah?

What happened to Lot's wife?

What did Lot's daughters do to preserve their lineage?

What two clans of people were created by their actions?

When they moved to Gerar in the Negev, how did Abraham describe his relationship to Sarah?

(Does this pretense sound familiar?)

What did King Abimelech do?

Who warned King Abimelech about Sarah's true identity?

What was Abraham's excuse for lying?

What was King Abimelech's response?

ISAAC
Genesis 21:1–25:18

> *After reading this section, you should be able to describe how God used Isaac. You should also be able to describe the character of this flawed human who was still useful to God.*

What promise did the Lord fulfill to Sarah?

How old was Abraham when Isaac was born?

What were Abraham and King Abimelech fighting over?

How was this dispute settled?

What happened at Isaac's weaning feast?
What was the result?
Why did this have to happen?

What was Abraham's response?

What did God do for Hagar and Ishmael?
What happened to Ishmael?

How did God test Abraham's faith?
Why was this request such an act of faith for Abraham?

> Something to think about: Try to put yourself in Abraham's shoes. Would you have had
> the faith of Abraham?

How did Abraham respond to God's request?

When God saw Abraham's faithful heart, what did He do?

Who was the most significant offspring of Nahor, Abraham's brother?

How old was Sarah when she died?
Where was Sarah buried?

(Locate this area on Map 21, "Abraham in Canaan.")

Why did Abraham insist Isaac's wife be chosen from his home country?

Who was chosen to be Isaac's wife?
Who did Abraham marry after Sarah's death?
How old was Abraham when he died?
Who buried Abraham?
Where was Abraham buried?
How old was Ishmael when he died?
What was the relationship between Isaac's and Ishmael's descendants?

> Something to think about: What is the relationship between these descendants today?

JACOB AND ESAU
Genesis 25:11–36:43

After reading this section, you should be able to describe how God used these two battling brothers to accomplish His plan.

Why did Isaac pray to God on Rebekah's behalf?

(Does this situation sound familiar?)

What was the result of Isaac's prayer?
What was the significance of the babies jostling in the womb?

Describe Esau.
Describe Jacob.
How was Esau's character demonstrated by his decision to sell his birthright to Jacob?

How was Jacob's character demonstrated by his scheme to get Esau's birthright?

What nation descended from Esau?

(Look at Map 21a, "Abraham, Isaac and Jacob." Trace Isaac's journey to Gerar.)

Why did Isaac move to Gerar?
Who was the king of the Philistines in Gerar?
What lie did Isaac tell about Rebekah?
Why did Isaac lie about his relationship to Rebekah?

(Does this sound familiar?)

How did God bless Isaac during this time?

How did the Philistines react to God's blessings on Isaac?

Where did Isaac finally settle?

(Locate this town on Map 21a.)

When Esau was forty years old, why did Isaac contact him?

While Esau was out hunting, what scheme did Rebekah devise?

What did Rebekah ask Jacob to do?

What was Isaac's reaction to Jacob?

What was Esau's reaction when he learned Jacob had stolen his blessing?

Why did Jacob go to Haran?

(Go to https://theologue.wordpress.com/2014/04/30/zaine-ridling-bible-atlas-e-book/. Look at Map 22, "Travels of Jacob.")

(Look at the map of the "Travels of Jacob." Locate Haran.)

Why did Isaac bless this plan for Jacob to leave Canaan?

What did Esau do out of spite toward Isaac?
While on his journey to Haran, what dream did Jacob have?

What was the significance of Jacob's dream?

Who did Jacob meet at the well in Haran?
What was Jacob's reaction to her?
How long did Laban tell Jacob he must work before he could marry Rachel?
What happened when the allotted time was up?

Discuss the irony of this event.

What compromise did Laban make with Jacob?

What was the result of Jacob loving Rachel more than Leah?

Discuss the irony of Jacob's unequal affection for his wives.

What sons were born to Leah?

What sons were born to Rachel's handmaiden, Bilhah?

What sons were born to Leah's handmaiden, Zilpah?

What did Rachel trade to Leah for a night with Jacob?

Who was born as a result?
Leah also gave birth to which son and daughter?
What son was finally born to Rachel?
Where did Jacob want to go?
What bargain was struck as Jacob's severance pay for his years of service to Laban?

How did Laban deceive Jacob?

How did Jacob trick Laban?
Describe the relationship between Jacob and Laban.

What was God's will for Jacob?
What was Jacob's response?

What did Rachel steal?
What threat did Jacob make concerning the thief?
Where did Rachel hide what she had stolen?

Why was Jacob so upset?

Why was Laban so upset?

What covenant agreement was reached?

What land did Jacob have to travel through to get to Canaan?
What action did Jacob take to prepare to meet Esau?

What happened to Jacob the night before he was to meet Esau?

Why did the man change Jacob's name to Israel?
What was Esau's reaction when he saw Jacob?

Why was Esau's response so surprising?

Where did Jacob finally settle his family?

(Locate this town on Map 22, "Travels of Jacob.")

What happened to Dinah?

How did Jacob's sons respond when they found out?
What marriage condition did Jacob set?

Three days later, what did Simeon and Levi do?

After becoming enemies of Shechem, where did God direct Jacob to go?

(Locate this town on Map 22, "Travels of Jacob.")

Why didn't anyone pursue Jacob?

What new name did God give to Jacob?

Something to think about: How is Jacob's new name significant even today?

What son was born to Rachel?
What happened to Rachel?
Name the twelve sons of Jacob (Israel). Include their mothers.

Where was Isaac when he died?
How old was Isaac when he died?
Who buried Isaac?
Where did Esau settle?
Esau became the father of what nation?

JOSEPH
Genesis 37:1–50:26

After reading this section, you should be able to describe how God used Joseph to accomplish His plan. You should also be able to describe the character of Joseph, which allowed him to be used by God.

How old was Joseph when he took time out from tending the flocks to tattle on his brothers?
What else caused Joseph to be hated by his brothers?

(Go to https://theologue.wordpress.com/2014/04/30/zaine-ridling-bible-atlas-e-book/. Look at Map 23, "The Journeys of Joseph.")

When Israel sent Joseph to check on his brothers, where did Joseph find them?

(Locate this area on Map 23, "The Journeys of Joseph.")

What did the brothers plot to do?
What plan did Reuben propose?
What did Reuben plan to do later?
What did the brothers (minus Reuben) do with Joseph?

How did the brother's fool Jacob/Israel?

What was Jacob/Israel's response to Joseph's loss?
Who bought Joseph from the Midianites?

(Look at Map 23, and trace Joseph's travels to Egypt.)

By Levirate law, what responsibility did Onan have to his dead brother, Er?

What did the Lord do to Onan because he broke this law?
In her quest to have children, how did Tamar deceive Judah?

What did Judah give Tamar as a pledge of payment?
When Tamar became pregnant and was accused of prostitution, what penalty did Judah demand?
How did Tamar avoid this punishment?
Who was born to Tamar?

> *Something to think about: Who would later descend through Perez in the line of Judah and Tamar?*

Why did Potiphar promote Joseph?

How did Joseph end up in prison?

Why did the warden put Joseph in charge of the other prisoners?

Which members of Pharaoh's staff landed in prison?
Who interpreted their dreams?
What was the interpretation of the cupbearer's dream?

What was the interpretation of the baker's dream?
Two years later when Pharaoh had a dream, who remembered Joseph's ability to interpret dreams?

Who did Joseph say would give Pharaoh the answer?
What was the interpretation of Pharaoh's dream?

What did Joseph propose to do about this?

Why did Potiphar put Joseph in charge?

Before the famine, which two sons were born to Joseph?
Why did Jacob send his sons from Canaan to Egypt?

Which brother did not make the trip to Egypt?
When Joseph recognized his brothers, of what did he accuse them?
What was Joseph's scheme?

What was Jacob's reaction to this plan?

What happened to change Jacob's mind?

What did Jacob/Israel send along?

What was Joseph's reaction when he saw Benjamin?

What scheme did Joseph come up with next?
Who begged for Benjamin and told Joseph the whole story?
What was Joseph's reaction to the story?
Why did Joseph say he was sent to Egypt?

What land did Pharaoh give to Joseph and the Israelites?
Who reassured Jacob/Israel about the move to Egypt?
How did people get food during the famine?

What was the first tax created by Joseph?

How long had the Israelites lived in Egypt?
How old was Jacob/Israel at this time?
Where did Jacob/Israel want to be buried?
Instead of blessing Joseph's firstborn son with his right hand, describe how Jacob/Israel blessed Manasseh and Ephraim.

As Jacob/Israel was about to die, what did he have to say about each of his sons?

Where did his sons bury Jacob/Israel?

Why were Joseph's brothers afraid?

What was Joseph's reaction to them?

When he died, where did Joseph want his bones to go?
How old was Joseph when he died?

A Nation Set Free

(1525–1400 BC)

> *In this section, identify how God's relationship is changing from a focus on individuals to the establishment of a relationship with a nation. Identify ways God used people and situations to carry out His plan. Be able to describe how God used Moses, a mere man, to mightily lead His people.*

MOSES AND THE ISRAELITES IN EGYPT
Exodus 1:1–6:27

Why was the new Egyptian king nervous?

What did the king do to oppress the Israelites?

What happened when the son of one of the Levite women became three months old and could no longer be kept hidden?
Who found the baby?
What was her reaction to the baby?

What name did she give to this baby? Why?

When he was grown, why did this man flee from Egypt?

Where did he go?
Who did he meet and marry?
How were the Israelites doing back in Egypt?
How did God respond to the plight of the Israelites?

What did Moses see while tending Jethro's flock?
Who spoke from this strange site?
What did He want?
Why was Moses reluctant to serve?

Put yourself in Moses's shoes. How would you have felt? What would you have done?

What miraculous signs did God give Moses as a demonstration of His power?

Why was Moses still reluctant?
What was God's response?

How did Zipporah save Moses's life?

How did the Israelites respond to God's plan?

THE PLAGUES
Exodus 5:1–11:10

How did Pharaoh respond to God's plan?

How old were Moses and Aaron at this time?
What happened when Pharaoh refused to believe in God's power even though Aaron's staff turned into a snake and ate the staff/snakes of the Egyptian magicians?

What was the first plague?
Why did Pharaoh refuse to let the Israelites go?
What was the second plague on the Egyptians?
Why did Pharaoh still refuse to let the Israelites go?

What was the third plague?
Why did Pharaoh continue to refuse to let the Israelites go?

Something to think about: Why did God harden Pharaoh's heart?

What was the fourth plague?
What was Pharaoh's response this time?

What was the fifth plague?
What was the sixth plague?

What was Pharaoh's response?
What was the seventh plague?

How did Pharaoh's response change?

What did God tell Moses about the purpose of the plagues?

What plague did Moses threaten next?
What was Pharaoh's response this time?
What was the eighth plague?
What was Pharaoh's response?

What was the ninth plague?

How did Pharaoh respond?
What was Moses's warning about the last plague?

What did God say Pharaoh's response would be?

THE PASSOVER AND THE EXODUS
Exodus 12:1–18:7

After reading this section, you should be able to give examples of how God directed and then protected His people. You should also be able to discuss why people seem to need constant reminders about who God is.

What ceremony did God institute?
When was this event to take place?
What were the Israelites told to do?

What feast was to follow? Describe the events.

Why was this feast established?

What happened in Egypt at midnight on the fourteenth day of the first month?

What was to be the Passover's significance to the Israelites?

What was Pharaoh's response after the Passover?

How did the Egyptians respond?

How many Israelite men left Egypt during the Exodus?

How long had the Israelites been in Egypt?
What day commemorated the Exodus?
Where were the Israelites headed?

When the Israelites arrived, what law was to be enacted?

Why did God lead the Israelites through the desert toward the Red Sea?

Whose bones did Moses bring along?
How did God guide the Israelites?
Why did God tell Moses to camp by the Red Sea?

Who pursued the Israelites? Why?
How did the Israelites respond when they saw the Egyptian army approaching?

What did Moses tell them?

What did the Lord tell Moses to do?

How did the Lord protect the Israelites during the night?

What else did the Lord do that night?

What happened when the Egyptians followed the Israelites into the Red Sea?

How did the Israelites respond when they saw what happened to the Egyptians?

(Go to http://www.bible-history.com/maps/route_exodus.html. Look at the map of the "Route of the Exodus of the Israelites from Egypt.")

> *Look for a recurring pattern of behavior as the*
> *Israelites travel through the desert.*

(Use the "Route of the Exodus of the Israelites from Egypt" to trace the journey of God's chosen nation through the Sinai.)

As Moses led the Israel nation through the Sinai and Negev deserts, what two things did they constantly grumble about?

How did God provide?

What special day was instituted?
How long did the Lord provide manna in the desert?

How did the Lord provide water at Horeb?

Who attacked the Israelites at Rephidim?
Who was the leader of Israel's army?
How did God provide the victory?

Who came to visit Moses?

What was Jethro's response when Moses told him all the good things God had done?

What process did Jethro suggest to help take pressure off Moses?

COVENANT ESTABLISHED
BETWEEN GOD AND ISRAEL
(1445 BC)
Exodus 19:1–31:18

> *Look for evidence of God's expectations for His people and His response when they fail Him.*

How long had the Israelites been in the desert?
Where did Moses meet with God?
What covenant did God propose?

What happened on "the morning of the third day"?

List the Ten Commandments.

What did God say He would do for those who love Him and keep His commandments?

Something to think about: What is the purpose of a reverent fear of God?

Who did God provide as a guide for the Israelites?
Who was summoned to worship God?

How long was Moses on the mountain receiving the tablets of stone on which the Ten Commandments were written?

(Go to www.knowingthebible.net/tabernacle-1444. Look at the photos of the tabernacle, the outer court, the Holy Place, the Most Holy Place, and God's presence in the temple. Click on the links in the narrative to view the photos.)
(Go to www.bible-history.com/art/tabrncl.htm. Look at photos of the furnishings of the tabernacle and a photo of the gems on the high priest's breastplate.)

Where did the Israelites get the supplies needed to build the tabernacle?

Who designed the tabernacle and its furnishings, dictated the priests' duties, and developed all the worship services?
Describe the ark of the covenant, including the mercy seat.

What was to be placed in the ark of the covenant?

Where was God to meet with Moses to give him His commands for the Israelites?

Describe the table for the bread of the Presence.
Describe the lampstand.
Describe the tabernacle.
How was the interior tabernacle space divided?

Describe the dimensions of the altar of burnt offerings.
Describe the dimensions of the outer court.

Who did God have anointed and ordained as priests?

How were the priests to dress?

> *Something to think about: What was the significance of the names of the twelve tribes of Israel being attached to the priestly garments?*

What two offerings were established?

What additional furnishing was added to the Holy Place? Describe it.

Why was a census offering established?
Describe the bronze laver. What was its use?

Why did God give such detailed instructions for worship?

What did the Lord give Moses after He finished giving him these detailed instructions for the tabernacle?

Covenant Broken
Exodus 32:1–33:23

> *Look for evidence of this recurring theme: "You shall be holy, as I am holy."*

What did the Israelites ask of Aaron while Moses was up on Mount Sinai with God?

How did Aaron respond to their request?

How did God respond?

How did Moses handle this grievous situation?

After Aaron denied responsibility, what story did he tell?

What happened to the Israelites as a result of their sin?

What went on in the Tent of Meeting?

What request did Moses make of the Lord?

> *Something to think about: Why was this call for God so important?*

How did God make this request happen?

Covenant Renewed
Exodus 34:1–35

How were the tablets of stone replaced?

Discuss how God's character was proclaimed to Moses on Mount Sinai.

Why did Moses put a veil over his face?

THE BUILDING OF THE TABERNACLE AND THE BEGINNING OF TEMPLE WORSHIP
Exodus 35:4–40:35

What structure was built to replace Moses's Tent of Meeting?
When was the tabernacle set up for the first time?

What was placed in the ark?
What happened when all the furnishings were in their proper places and the courtyard was set up around the tabernacle?

THE ESTABLISHMENT OF PRIESTS AND INSTRUCTIONS FOR TEMPLE WORSHIP
Leviticus 8:1–10:20; Numbers 3:1–8:22

Who did God tell Moses to ordain as priests?
Why was God's choice of Aaron somewhat surprising?

What did His choice demonstrate about God's nature?
What consumed the burnt offering on the altar?

What did Nadab and Abihu do that was so displeasing to God?

What was their punishment?
What command did the Lord give to Aaron and his sons?

What three priests were left after Nadab and Abihu's unauthorized use of fire?

What tribe was designated by God to assist the priests?

Discuss why this tribe might have been chosen for this particular assignment.

What duties were they to perform?

What was the age of duty for men given this special task?
When did the offerings begin?

Who was responsible for bringing the offering?

List the tribes in the order of their offering.

Describe what was offered.

Where did the Lord's voice come from when He spoke to Moses in the Tent of Meeting?

THE ESTABLISHMENT OF NEW LAWS
Numbers 9:1–12, 1:1–4:49

Think about why laws are now necessary.

How long had the Israelites been in the desert?
When was the Passover to be celebrated?
What problem did some of the Israelites have that kept them from celebrating the Passover?

What did the Lord tell Moses to do about this problem?

Discuss how God's decision demonstrated His character.

When did the numbering of the Israelite nation take place?
Who was being counted?
Why was this census being taken?

Discuss why Israel might need an army.

Who was to help with this census?
What was the final tally?
Which families were not counted in this census?
Why weren't they included in this census?

Which tribe was the largest?
How were the Israelites instructed to set up their camp?

What count was made of the Levites?
What tabernacle responsibility did the Gershonites have?

What tabernacle responsibility did the Kohathites have?

What tabernacle responsibility did the Merarites have?

Who were the only two people who could enter the sanctuary?
What additional responsibility did the Kohathites have?

What temple tax was assessed?

THE JOURNEY THROUGH THE DESERT
(1445 BC–1406 BC)
Numbers 10:1–33:7

> *In this section, be prepared to describe the ways in which God continually provided for His people. Be able to identify a recurring pattern of behavior by the Israelites and be able to give examples of how God repeatedly responded to His chosen nation.*

What was the significance of the sounding of the silver trumpets?

When did the Israelites set out from the Sinai Desert?

Who did Moses ask to guide them through the desert?
How did the Lord lead the Israelites on their journey?

What caused the complaining to begin?

How did Moses respond?

How did the Lord respond to Moses's call for help?

How did the Lord respond to the people's cry for meat?
Why were Miriam and Aaron upset with Moses?

What was Miriam's punishment for disrespecting Moses?

Discuss what this event revealed about Moses's relationship with God.

When the Israelites reached the land of Canaan, what was the first order of business?

How long were the spies in the land of Canaan?

Upon returning, what was their report?

Which two spies disagreed with this report?
How did these two men respond to the lack of faith demonstrated by the Israelites?

What was the Lord's response?

What was Moses's argument for mercy?

What was the Lord's judgment on the Israelites?

What happened when the Israelites admitted their sin and tried to enter the Promised Land without the Lord?

Something to think about: How might this event and these outcomes apply to God's followers today?

Who rose up to challenge the leadership of Moses and the priesthood of Aaron?

How did the Lord deal with this act of rebellion?

How many died before Aaron made atonement?

What test did the Lord use to prove Aaron was His chosen one?

Who was given the priesthood responsibility as their service to the Lord?

Who were the only ones allowed to enter the sanctuary (Holy of Holies)?
Who was given the task of assisting the priests?
How were the priests and Levites to be supported in the Promised Land?

Who died at Kadesh?
What problem arose in the Desert of Zin?
What instruction did God give Moses as a solution to this problem?

What did Moses and Aaron do instead?

How did God punish Moses and Aaron?

Discuss why Moses and Aaron were punished.

(Go to www.bible-history.com/maps/canaanite_nations.html. Look at the "Map of Canaanite Nations" to see who inhabited the Promised Land at this time.)

Whose land did the Israelites have to cross?
What happened when Moses made his request to cross peacefully?

Who died on Mount Hor?
Who replaced this man?
Who attacked the Israelites along the road to Atharim?
Who won? Why?
While traveling along the route to the Red Sea to avoid going through Edom, what caused the Israelites to start to grumble again?
How did the Lord respond to their unfaithfulness?

How did the Lord respond to Moses's prayers for the people?

Who fought with the Israelites at Jahaz?
Who won? Why?
Who else was defeated by the Israelites?

Discuss the significance of the details provided by Moses in his journal of the exodus from Egypt and of the Israelites' forty-years of wandering through the wilderness.

Where were the Israelites camped before they entered the Promised Land?

Why was King Balak of the Moabites so terrified?

Who did King Balak summon for help?

Why was this request refused at first?

What did King Balak do next?
What was Balaam's response?

Why was God angered?

Why did the donkey on which Balaam was riding suddenly turn off the road and go into the field?

What was Balaam's response?
When the path was blocked again, what did the donkey do?

What was Balaam's response?
When the path was blocked for a third time, what did the donkey do?

> *Think about it: Has the Lord ever put an angel in your path or used a donkey to oppose a potential action on your part? Were you able to see the angel? Did you recognize the donkey? Why or why not? What was the outcome?*

What was Balaam's response this third time?
Who rebuked Balaam for his violent actions?
Who also rebuked Balaam?

How did Balaam respond?
How did God use Balaam?
What did Balaam deliver to King Balak?

What sin problem arose while the Israelite nation was camped at Shittim?

Discuss how ungodly relationships can influence one's spiritual life.

What was the Israelites' punishment?

How did Eleazar's son and the priest, Phinehas, respond?

What was the Midianites' severe punishment?

Why was a second census taken?

Compare each tribe's total numbers with those from the first census taken forty years earlier. Which tribes are larger? Which are smaller? What was the status of the Levites? How many fighting men were there? Who were the only two fighting men left from the first count? Why?

JOSHUA, ISRAEL'S NEW LEADER
Numbers 27:15–23, 32:1–35:8
Deuteronomy 4: 41-43

Why was Joshua chosen to succeed Moses as the leader of the Israelite nation?

(Go to https://theologue.wordpress.com/2014/04/30/zaine-ridling-bible-atlas-e-book/. Look at Map 39, "The Tribal Allotments of Israel.")

Which tribes asked Moses to be allowed to settle east of the Jordan River?

What did Moses suspect was their motivation?

What were their reasons?
What promise did they make?

Why did Moses set aside three cities east of the Jordan?

What directives did Moses give to the Israelites in preparation for conquering the Promised Land?

> *Discussion: Why was it so important not to allow any enemies to remain? What implication does this rationale have for today's followers of God?*

What other action did the Lord tell Moses to take?

What allotment was given to the Levites?

MOSES'S REVIEW OF ISRAELITE HISTORY
Deuteronomy 1:1–11:32

> *As you read through this section, think about why Moses felt it was so important to leave the Israelites with these final thoughts. Also think about how some of his key points might apply in your spiritual life today.*

Where was Moses when he delivered the first of his two final addresses to the Israelite nation?

How long has it been since the Israelites left Egypt?

Briefly summarize the key points of Moses's first address.

In his second address to the Israel nation, what was the first point made by Moses?

From where did the law come?
What purpose did the law fulfill?

What was the first and most important commandment?

How were the laws to be passed from generation to generation?

What directive did Moses give about how God wanted their defeated enemies to be treated?

Why did God choose the Israelites to be His people, His treasured possession?

How were the Israelites told they would be able to defeat the nations currently occupying Canaan?

Why were the Israelites tested in the desert for forty years?

What did Moses warn might happen as they prospered in the Promised Land?

What evidence did Moses have that this might happen?

In summary, what was God's will for the Israelite nation?

On what were God's blessings contingent?

The Laws of Moses

(1450–1400 BC)

> *Think about why Israel needed laws at this time. Be able to identify the purpose of these laws and to state what punishment was to be carried out if they were broken.*

RELIGIOUS LAWS
Exodus, Leviticus, Numbers, and Deuteronomy

Who was the source of these laws?

What were these laws designed to do?

What was the first and most important commandment?

What was the second commandment?

What heinous activity was practiced by some idol worshippers?

What was the punishment for idolatry?

Where were the Israelites told to go to worship the Lord?

What false spiritualists' activities were prohibited?

What was to be done with those who practiced these activities?

How were the Israelites to know who the true prophets were?

What was the third commandment?

What was the penalty for breaking this commandment?

Why did God require certain gifts and tithes to be given?

What was the fourth commandment?

What was the penalty for working on the Sabbath?

List the three major feasts and the one special day established by God. Describe each one. Include when each was observed, what was signified, and what the penalty was for nonobservance.

What other one-day feast was established?

What was the purpose of specific sacrifices and offerings?

What forms did the five main sacrifices and offerings take?

List some of the special offerings that were required.

List the rules that governed an offering.

What other rituals had to be observed?

What rules were given to the priests?

Discuss why these laws of cleanliness and holiness were so important.

What was the purpose of the sabbatical year?

What was the Year of Jubilee?

Under what conditions was a person deemed "unclean"?

Why was purification necessary?

Who was forbidden to enter the Lord's assembly?

Describe the Nazarite vow. What was its purpose?

What were "vows of dedication"?

To maintain their separateness as a holy nation, what were the Israelites not allowed to combine?

LAWS OF GOVERNMENT
Deuteronomy 17:14–20

Who was to be the Israelites' supreme leader?
What did God anticipate the Israelites would want once they took possession of the Promised Land?

What stipulations did God place on this office?

Discuss why God put these limitations in place.

JUDICIAL LAWS
Exodus, Numbers, and Deuteronomy

Describe the judicial system as developed by God.

What stipulations were placed on all judges? Why?

What was the ninth commandment?
What was the penalty for giving false testimony?

How many witnesses were required for a conviction?

Discuss why this law was so important and why it still applies today.

What limitations were placed on punishments?

CRIMINAL LAWS
Exodus, Leviticus, Numbers, and Deuteronomy

As you read through this section, think about the harshness of the penalties for breaking these laws and why such punishment was necessary.

What was the sixth commandment?
What was the penalty for premeditated, intentional murder?
What was the penalty for manslaughter or unintentional murder?

List the penalty for each of the following crimes:
Causing a miscarriage
Kidnapping
Bodily harm
Rape
Assault
What was the eighth commandment?
What was the penalty for theft?

CIVIL LAWS AND LAWS GOVERNING
PERSONAL BEHAVIOR
Exodus, Leviticus, Numbers, and Deuteronomy

What was the purpose of civil laws?

Discuss the purpose of today's civil laws.

List the penalty for each of the following crimes:
Negligence
Arson
Crop damage by livestock
Bodily harm by livestock
What laws governed the master/slave relationship?

What laws governed credit, charging interest, and collateral on loans?

How were contracts and agreements to be guaranteed?

What character trait was supposed to govern all business dealings?
Who was designated as the legal heir?
If a man died without an heir, what was his brother's obligation?

Under what condition could a daughter inherit?

If a woman was assumed to be a virgin before marriage and later was found not to be, what was the punishment?
Was divorce allowed?
What was the seventh commandment?
What was the penalty for violation of this commandment?

How did the Lord feel about prostitution?
What was the penalty for incest?

What was the penalty for homosexuality and bestiality?
How did God describe sins of a sexual nature?

LAWS GOVERNING HEALTH AND
THE GENERAL WELFARE
Exodus, Leviticus, and Deuteronomy

Why did God provide regulations for certain health conditions?

Discuss the purpose of today's health regulations.

Why did God prohibit the Israelites from eating certain foods or from coming in contact with certain creatures, including dead animals?

When God gave the Israelites specific laws governing their treatment of others, what do you think His intent was?

What was the fifth commandment?
Why was this commandment so important?

What was the penalty for disrespecting parents?
How were the elderly to be treated?
How were neighbors to be treated?

What was the tenth commandment?
Why was this commandment so important?

LAWS GOVERNING WARFARE
Deuteronomy 20:1–20, 23:9–14

Who did God say was the "commander-in-chief" of the Israelite army?

Before attacking a city, what did God command the Israelites to do?

Why did God direct the Israelites to kill every member of the nations inhabiting their Promised Land?

When laying siege to a city, what trees were to be spared? Why?

According to Deuteronomy 24:5, how long was a newly married soldier exempt from service?

Discuss some possible reasons for this law.

PERSONAL RESPONSIBILITIES WITHIN THESE LAWS
Leviticus 22:31–33; 26:3–46; Deuteronomy 12:32; 31:9–13; Numbers 15:37–41

What was required of all Israelites?

Discuss why a personal commitment to God's law is so important and necessary.

What was the function of the tassels attached by a blue cord to the corners of the Israelites' garments?

How else were the Israelites to be reminded about God's laws?

If obedient, what blessings would the Israelites enjoy?

If disobedient, what punishment would the Israelites face?

The Israelites' Arrival in Canaan: The Beginning of Life in the Promised Land

(1400–1100 BC)

THE RENEWAL OF THE COVENANT BETWEEN GOD AND ISRAEL
Deuteronomy 26:16–19, 28:1–30:20

If the Israelites chose to obey God, what blessings did the Lord promise?

If the Israelites chose not to follow God's covenant, what punishment did the Lord guarantee?

With whom did God make His covenant?

What happened if God's people repented of their sins?
What two basic choices did the Israelites have?

JOSHUA'S LEADERSHIP
Deuteronomy 31:1–33:29

How old was Moses when he stepped down as Israel's leader?
Who did God commission as the next leader of the Israel nation?
Why do you think God chose this man?

What happened to the book of the laws of Moses?

Why did God give Moses a song?

List the key messages found in this song.

MOSES'S DEATH
Deuteronomy 34:1–12

Where did God tell Moses to go on his last day?

Why did God send Moses here?

What was Moses's last official act?

What tribute was paid to Moses after his death?

(Go to www.bible-history.com/maps/canaanite_nations.html. Look back at the "Map of Canaanite Nations" to see who inhabited the Promised Land.)

(Go to https://theologue.wordpress.com/2014/04/30/zaine-ridling-bible-atlas-e-book/. Look at Map 36, "Joshua's Central and Southern Campaigns," and Map 37, "Joshua's Northern Campaign.")

THE CONQUEST OF CANAAN
(1406–1390 BC?)
The Book of Joshua

> *Use the maps of the Canaanite nations and Joshua's campaigns to track the progress of the Israelites conquest of the Promised Land. Look for all the times when God shows His awesome power and think about His purpose in these demonstrations of omnipotence.*

How much time had passed since God first promised Canaan to the Israelites?

List the key points in God's final instructions to Joshua.

How many spies were sent? To what city were they sent?

Where did the spies seek shelter?

What happened when the king of Jericho found out about the spies?

After receiving a promise of safety for Rahab and her family, what happened to the spies?

What was given as a sign of their promise of safety?

What was the spies' report this time?

What led the way as the Israelite nation moved from the plains of Moab into the Promised Land?

How did God demonstrate His power when the Israelites reached the Jordan River?

What did the Israelites build at Gilgal?

What was the significance of this structure?

How did the Amorite and Canaanite kings react when they heard what the Lord had done to the Jordan River?

Name four important events that occurred before the Israelites attacked Jericho.

Describe how the Israelites were able to take the city of Jericho.

What specific instructions were given on the seventh day? Why?

Who disobeyed one of God's instructions?

What happened as a result of this sin?

How was this situation rectified?

How were the Israelites able to conquer Ai on the second attempt?

How did Joshua and the Israelites honor God?

When the kings west of the Jordan heard about the Israelites' victories at Jericho and Ai, what was their reaction?
What trick did the Gibeonites pull on Joshua? Why?

Why did this trick work?
What happened when the truth was learned?

Name the five kings of the Amorites.

What was their response when they heard about the peace treaty between the Israelites and the Gibeonites?
How did God assist in the Israelites' victory at Gibeon?

What amazing feat did God perform on this day?

What happened to the five kings of the Amorites and to their cities?

How did the northern kings respond when they heard how the Israelites had defeated the southern kings?

How was the Israelite army able to defeat so great an enemy?
How many kings were conquered and killed by Joshua and the Israelites?

(Go to https://theologue.wordpress.com/2014/04/30/zaine-ridling-bible-atlas-e-book/. Look at Map 39, "The Tribal Allotments of Israel." Use this map to determine the land given to each tribe.)

Who inherited the Promised Land?

Who made the decision about how the land was to be divided?
What land was inherited by the other two and one-half tribes?

Why did the tribe of Levi inherit no land?

Who was granted a special request as his inheritance? Why?

What tribe received the first allotment of land?
Who received the next allotments?

After the remaining land was surveyed, how was the order of its division determined by the rest of the tribes?

What did the Israelites give Joshua?

(Go to https://theologue.wordpress.com/2014/04/30/zaine-ridling-bible-atlas-e-book/. Look at Map 40, "Levitical Cities and Cities of Refuge." Use this map to locate the towns mentioned.)

What special cities were set up? Why?

How many Levitical cities were there?
Explain how God kept His covenant with Israel.

List the main points of Joshua's address to the soldiers from the eastern tribes of Israel.

What was Joshua's message to the western tribes?

How did Joshua begin his farewell address at Shechem?

Discuss why Joshua began his message in this way.

What did Joshua challenge the Israelites to do?

How did the Israelites respond?

JOSHUA'S DEATH
(1390 BC?)
Joshua 24:29–33; Judges 2:8–9

How old was Joshua when he died?
Where was he buried?

Who else died at this time?
Who else was buried at Shechem?

THE PERIOD OF THE JUDGES
(1400–1058 BC?)
Joshua 13–17; Judges 1–12

> *As you read through this section, look for times when obedience resulted in prosperity and disobedience led to adversity. Also take note of how God always remained faithful to His covenant.*

Which tribe was sent out to fight the Canaanites first?

Which tribe was asked to help in the fight?

What was the punishment for King Adoni-Bezek, a Canaanite? Why?

Why were God's people unable to drive these foreigners from the plains?

What specific God-given order regarding the conquest of the Promised Land did the Israelites fail to obey?
Give some examples of their failure to comply.

What was the consequence of this act of disobedience?

Explain how this new generation of Israelites' experience with God was different from that of their forefathers?

> *God's chosen nation falls into a predictable behavioral cycle, i.e., Israel is faithful—rejects God as King—becomes disobedient and turns away from God—is forsaken by God—is conquered and enslaved—cries out to God—becomes repentant and turns back to God—is delivered by God—becomes faithful again. Look for evidence of this pattern as you read through this section.*

What sin separated the Israelites from God?
What were the consequences of this sin?

How did God use the Israelites' enemies?

How did the Israelites perform in this area?

JUDGES OF ISRAEL

Name	Length of Service	Notes

(As you study, fill in the "Judges of Israel Chart.")

(Go to https://theologue.wordpress.com/2014/04/30/zaine-ridling-bible-atlas-e-book/. Use Map 41, "The Judges of Israel," to help identify who served where and when.)

Who was the first judge raised up by God to serve as a deliverer of His people?

(Go to https://theologue.wordpress.com/2014/04/30/zaine-ridling-bible-atlas-e-book/. Look at Map 42, "Ehud and the Oppression of the Moabites.")

After eighteen years of oppression, who delivered the Israelites from King Eglon and the Moabites?

Describe how this judge was able to kill King Eglon.

Who saved Israel from the Philistines? How?

(Go to https://theologue.wordpress.com/2014/04/30/zaine-ridling-bible-atlas-e-book/. Look at Map 43, "Deborah's Victory over the Canaanites.")

What prophetess was raised up as a judge of Israel?
Who was the commander-in-chief of Israel's army?
Who was the commander of King Jabin's Canaanite army?
What stipulation was placed on Barak's involvement in the attack on the Canaanite army?

What was the result of this special request?

How did the Canaanite general respond when the Lord routed his troops?

Who offered a hiding place to the Canaanite general?
What happened to the Canaanite general?

How long was there peace in the land?

(Go to https://theologue.wordpress.com/2014/04/30/zaine-ridling-bible-atlas-e-book/. Look at Map 44, "Gideon's Battles with the Amalekites.")

Because Israel did evil in the sight of the Lord, what nation was allowed to become her oppressor?

How long did this oppression go on?
Describe how the Israelites were oppressed.

Who did God call on to save Israel?
What was this man's initial response?

What was the Lord's response?

What sign was given?

That same night, what did the Lord ask Gideon to do?

Why did Gideon do as the Lord requested, but at night?

Still unsure of God's support, what tests did Gideon request from God?

Describe how God chose the number of fighting men He wanted for the Israelites' battle against the Midianites and their allies.

Why did God reduce the number of fighting men?

Describe the strength of the army amassed by the Midianites, Amalekites, and all the other eastern peoples.

What event gave Gideon great confidence in this battle?

Describe the attack on the Midianite camp.

Why were the men of the cities of Succoth and Peniel punished after Gideon captured the Midianite kings?

After the victory, what position did the Israelites offer to Gideon?
What was Gideon's response?

How long was the land at peace?

What happened to Israel after Gideon died?

Who set himself up as king by killing his seventy brothers?

Who escaped the killings?

How did God deal with this evil "king"?

How did this evil "king" meet his demise?

(Go to https://theologue.wordpress.com/2014/04/30/zaine-ridling-bible-atlas-e-book/. Look at Map 45, "Jephthah and the Ammonites.")

Who was the next judge of Israel?

How long was his term?

Who was the next judge?

How long was his term?

What happened to Israel after this judge's term ended?

What did Israel do to get back into the Lord's favor?

Who did the elders of Gilead ask to command the Israelite army in their battle against the Ammonites?

What vow did this commander make before God in return for a victory?

What was the result of this vow?

How long did this warrior/judge lead Israel?

Who was the next judge?

How long was his term?

Who was next?

How long was his term?

Who was next?

How long was his term?

THE STORY OF RUTH
(1100 BC)
The Book of Ruth

Look for evidence of Ruth's faithfulness.

Who was Elimelech?

Why did he take his family to Moab?
Who did the two sons marry?
What happened to the men of the family?
What prompted Naomi to return to Judah?

Why did Naomi encourage her daughters-in-law to stay?

Who insisted on going with Naomi? Why?

Once they reached Bethlehem, how was food to be provided?

In whose field did Ruth gather grain?
How was Ruth treated?

What was Ruth's reputation?
How did the Lord reward Ruth's faithfulness?

How was Ruth related to David?

SAMSON

(1090–1050 BC?)

Judges 13–16

> *In this section, look for evidence of how easily an*
> *evil influence can corrupt a good person.*

After a lapse into evil behavior, into whose hands did the Lord deliver the Israelites?

How long did this oppression last?
What did the angel of the Lord promise to Manoah's wife?

What was this child's name?
Even though he was from the tribe of Dan, who did he want for a wife?

What happened as he and his parents journeyed to Timnah?

What happened when they returned for the wedding?

What riddle was told at the wedding feast?

What was the prize if the riddle was solved during the seven days of the wedding feast?

How was the riddle solved?

What happened when the riddle's answer was revealed?

What revenge was taken on the Philistines when her father refused to let Samson visit his wife?

What did the Philistines do to get even?
What was the result of this vicious act?

> *Discuss the consequences of seeking vengeance.*

Why did the men of Judah come to the cave in the rock of Etam?

What happened when the prisoner transfer was about to take place?

What happened at Gaza?

With whom did Samson fall in love?
What did the Philistine rulers want this woman to do?

What three lies did he tell her? What was the result of each lie?

What finally caused the secret of great strength to be revealed?

What was the secret source of Samson's great strength?

What happened when the source was destroyed?

What did the Philistines do to Samson?

What was Samson's final act of revenge?

Discuss how Samson's weakness for the wrong type of woman affected his life. How can the life lessons of this story be applied today?

How long did Samson lead Israel?

(Judges 17–21)

What did Micah set up in his home in the hill country of Ephraim?

Why was it possible for Micah to take this action?

Who did Micah hire as his priest?
Who came to spy out the hill country of Ephraim?

What did these people want?
What happened when the five spies and six hundred men armed for battle arrived at Micah's house?

What happened at Laish?

Who did these people worship?
Who journeyed from his father-in-law's house in Bethlehem, Judah, to Gibeah in Benjamin?

Why were these people forced to spend the night in the city square?

Who finally offered hospitality to the travelers?

Who showed up to cause trouble?
What did they want?
What was offered instead but refused?
Who was sent out to satisfy these men?
What happened to this woman?

What did the Levite do to seek justice for his concubine?

How did the Israelites respond to this awful incident?

Describe the number of troops involved in this battle.

Who won the first day's battle?
Who won the second day's battle?
What did the men of Israel do?

What was the Lord's response?

What happened on the third day of battle?

Discuss why there was such a moral decline amongst the Israelites during the period of the judges. What pattern of behavior was repeatedly demonstrated by the Israelite nation during this time?

The Kings of Israel

(1100–930 BC)

> In this section, look for parallels between Elkanah and Hannah and Abraham and Sarah. Also, look for examples of how choices determine outcomes.

SAMUEL AS GOD'S SERVANT
1 Samuel 1:1–7:17

KINGS OF ISRAEL AND JUDAH

Kings of Israel	Length of Reign	*Dates (B.C.)	Good or Bad?

Kings of Judah	Length of Reign	*Dates (B.C.)	Good or Bad?

*Dates taken from Rose Book of Bible Charts, Maps &
Time Lines, Rose Publishing, 2005, pg. 64.

(As you study, fill in the chart of the "Kings of Israel.")

Who was Elkanah?

Name his wives.

What was the problem between these two wives?

What vow did Hannah make to the Lord?

Who witnessed this vow?
What did this man think was going on?

How did the Lord answer Hannah's prayer?

What did Hannah do with this boy?

Describe the character of the priest's sons.

Because she gave Samuel to God, how did the Lord bless Hannah?

Describe Samuel's character.
What did the man of God say would happen to his sons as a result of Eli's lack of discipline?

Discuss what can happen when discipline is lacking.

Describe how God called Samuel.

In what position did God place Samuel?

Who attacked and defeated the Israelites?
What did they steal?
What happened when Eli heard the news?

How long had Eli led Israel?
What happened in the enemy's cities as a result of the theft?

How long did it take before the enemy wanted to return what had been stolen?
How was it returned?

When the stolen artifact was returned, what happened to seventy Israelites when they looked inside?

What had to be done before God would deliver the Israelites from the hand of the Philistines?

Where did Samuel call home?
What motivated the Israelite elders to ask Samuel for a king?

How did God feel about this request?
What warning did Samuel give Israel about life in a monarchy?

How did the Israelites respond?

Who did God choose to be Israel's first king?
Who was this man?

Discuss the significance of this man's tribal affiliation.

Why was this man seeking Samuel's counsel?

What was his response when told Israel wanted him to lead them?

Discuss a time when you reacted in this same way.

What signs did Samuel give to reassure this man?

What happened to this future king when he turned to leave Samuel?

When Samuel called all the tribes of Israel together to introduce their new king, what was His Highness doing?
When the Ammonites attacked Jabesh Gilead, what did they demand as a treaty condition?

How did the new Israelite king respond?

Why did Samuel give the Israelites another history lesson during his farewell address?

Think about other Israelite leaders who gave farewell addresses.

What did Samuel say it took to please God?

Discuss how this teaching applies today.

KING SAUL
(1043?–1011 BC)
1 Samuel 8:1–15:35
1 Chronicles 5: 10, 18-22

How old was Saul when he became Israel's first king?
Describe Saul's immediate family.

How long did Saul reign?
Who was the commander of Saul's army?
What enemy was Saul preparing to battle at Micmash?
Describe the troop makeup of the two opposing armies.

How did the men of Israel react when they saw the strength of the opposing army?

Why was Saul waiting for Samuel?

Instead of waiting patiently and faithfully, what did Saul do?

What did this decision demonstrate about Saul's heart?

What was the result of Saul's disobedience?

Who went out to attack one of the Philistine outposts?
What was the attitude of this soldier as he planned his attack?

What was the result of this attack?

What order did Saul give to his soldiers?

Who violated Saul's order?
What was his reason for ignoring Saul's order?

What happened when this act of disobedience was discovered?

Why were the eastern tribes successful in their war against the Hagrites?

Why did God send the Israelites to attack the Amalekites?

What was the objective of this mission?
What decision did Saul make with regard to this objective?

When confronted by Samuel, what did Saul say was the reason for his disobedience?

What was Samuel's response?

What was Saul's excuse?

How did Samuel and the Lord feel about Saul as king?

DAVID AND HIS PSALMS
1 Samuel 16:1–2 Samuel 1:27

As you read this section, make a list of David's character traits and think about how these qualities made him a "man after God's own heart."

Who did the Lord choose to be Saul's successor?
Under what pretense did Samuel travel to Bethlehem? Why?

When choosing a king, what did Samuel consider that made him just like all other men?

What did the Lord consider when choosing a king?
Many men passed in front of Samuel, but who did the Lord want anointed as the next king of Israel?

Describe this man.

As a sign of his lost favor with God, what had departed from Saul?
What took its place?
How could his tormented spirit be relieved?
Where did Saul find such a person? Who was he?
Who gathered their forces for war against the Israelites?
Who was their champion?
Describe him.

What deal did he offer the Israelites?

How did Saul and all the other Israelites react to this challenge?
How long did this confrontation go on?
What did Saul offer to anyone who would kill the Philistine's champion?

Who stepped up to meet this challenge?
What were his qualifications to fight?

Describe his weapons.

> Discussion: What did David mean when he said, "It is not by sword or spear that the Lord saves" (1 Samuel 17:47)?

How did this confrontation end?

Who befriended David?

How did Saul react to David's newfound popularity?

Why did Saul want David to become his son-in-law?

What happened when David went to get Saul's asking price for his daughter's hand in marriage?

Why did Saul harden his heart toward David?

How did Jonathan intercede for David?

What was the result?
After another victory over the Philistines, how did Saul react?

How did Michal help David escape?

(Go to https://theologue.wordpress.com/2014/04/30/zaine-ridling-bible-atlas-e-book/. Use Map 50, "David's Flight from Saul," to track David's escape routes.)

To whom did David run?
How did David express his emotions during these difficult situations? Read Psalm 59.

Discuss how music helps soothe the soul.

Who came to kill David?
How did God protect David?
Who made a covenant with David, promising to provide inside information about King Saul's murderous intentions?
What feast was David afraid to attend?
What was the king's reaction to David's empty seat at the table?

How did Jonathan feel about his father's intentions?

Why did Saul say he wanted to kill David?
What communication method did Jonathan and David develop as a warning system?

Describe the relationship between Jonathan and David.

While on the run, where did David get bread?

Who else was present that day?
What weapon did David take?
What prayer of confidence did David write when seized by the Philistines? Read Psalm 56.

How did David avoid the threat of King Achish and the Philistines?

Read each psalm aloud as it is noted in this section.

Why did David write Psalm 34?
Where did David flee next?
Who came to support him?

What prayer did David pen while in this place? Read Psalm 142.
Who defected to join David's raiding band? (1 Chronicles 12: 8 – 18)

Where did David send his parents for safekeeping?
How did David know it was time to move on?

Where did David go next?
Who informed Saul about David's movements at Nob?
Who paid with their lives?

How did David find out about this slaughter?

What did David do when he learned of the killings? Read Psalm 52

God gave the Philistines into David's hand and saved what town?
Who pursued David and his men at this place?
How did David know to flee from this town?

Where did David and his army go next?

Why did David write Psalm 63?
Who came to see David at Horesh?
What aid did this man provide?
Who plotted with Saul against David?
Why did David write Psalm 54?

How did David and his men narrowly escape Saul and his army?

Where did David and his forces go next?
Where were they hiding?
Who entered?
Why did this man enter?
What did his men encourage David to do?
What did David do instead?
What rebuke did David give to his men?
When confronted by David, what was the man's response?

Why did David write Psalm 57?

Who died?
Where was he buried?
While in the Desert of Maon, to whom did David go for provisions?

What was the man's response when asked for aid?

What was David's response?

Who prepared provisions and intervened, pleading for mercy?

The next morning when the man was sober and his wife told him what she had done, what happened?

Who did David ask to become one of his wives?

While David and his men were in the Desert of Ziph, who came after them again?

Who secretly entered the enemy's camp at night?
How was this possible?
What did David have the opportunity to do?
Why didn't he?

What did David do instead?

What was King Saul's response?

Where did David and his men go next?
How long did David stay here?

What was so special about the warriors who came to join David's army? (1 Chronicles 12: 1-7)

What was David's standing policy whenever he attacked an area?

Who wanted David's army to fight with his?
What position did this man give David?
What happened the first time all the Philistines gathered to attack the Israelites at Jezreel?

What was the status of David's army at this time? (1 Chronicles 12: 19-22)

What happened in Ziklag while David and his army were gone?

What was the reaction of these brave, fighting men?

How did David handle this situation?

Who helped David find the Amalekite raiding party?

What happened when David's army attacked this raiding party?

What issue arose when the four hundred who went to fight returned to the resting place of the two hundred who were too exhausted to follow?

What new statute did David establish to handle this situation?
When Saul was afraid of the strength of the Philistine army assembled at Shunem, whom did he first ask for help?
Who did he consult next?
Whose spirit did he ask her to conjure up?
What was this spirit's prophecy?

Where did this battle between the Philistines and the Israelites take place? (1 Chronicles 10: 1-12)
Who was killed?
How did King Saul die?

What did the Philistines do with the bodies of Saul and his sons?

What did the Philistines do with Saul's armor?

Who retrieved the bodies?
Why did Saul die?

When news about his father's death came to Jezreel, what happened to Mephibosheth, Jonathan's five-year-old son?
How did David learn about the deaths of Saul and Jonathan?

How did David and his men react when they heard the news?

What key question did David ask this young man?

What was the result of his answer?

KING DAVID

(1011–971 BC)

2 Samuel 1: 1-24:25; 1 Chronicles 11: 1 – 2 Chronicles 1: 1; David's Psalms

When David asked, where did the Lord tell him to go?
What happened to David after he settled his family here?

Who did Abner, the commander of Saul's army, set up as king over Israel? How old was he?
How long did he reign?
What happened when the two sides met at the pool of Gibeon?

(Go to https://theologue.wordpress.com/2014/04/30/zaine-ridling-bible-atlas-e-book/. Use Map 52, "David's Wars of Conquest," to follow the battles described in this section.)

How did the two commanders decide to begin the battle?

How did this turn out?
What do we know about Asahel?
Who did Asahel target in the battle?
How did this turn out?

Who sought revenge?
What brought this fight to a halt?

Which army was winning this civil war?

Name the sons born to David while he lived in Hebron.

What accusation did Ish-Bosheth make against Abner?

What was Abner's reaction?

What condition did David place on their meeting?

What was the result of this meeting?

How did Joab, David's army commander, react when he heard about this meeting?

Why did Abner return to Hebron?
What happened to Abner?

How did David react when he heard the news?

What happened to Ish-Bosheth?

What was David's reaction when Baanah and Recab came to Hebron?

What happened when all the elders of Israel came to King David at Hebron?

How old was David? How long was his reign?

Approximately how many warriors from the thirteen tribes came to Hebron to join David's army?

What city did they capture first?
Once taken, what was this city called?
Who had a palace built for King David?
What did David want to bring back to his city?

Why was Uzzah killed?

How did David feel about the Lord's response?

Who came to attack the Israelites again?
Where did these battles take place?

Why was the Israelite army successful?

Why did David write Psalm 18?

What did David prepare for the ark?
Who did David commission to transport the ark this time?

Describe the atmosphere as the ark was brought to the City of David.

Who was not celebrating?

Why did David write Psalms 96 and 105?

Make a list of David's officials.

How did King David pay homage to Jonathan?

What building project did David wish to undertake?

How did the Lord respond?

What was David's response when Nathan told him what the Lord had said?

(Go to https://theologue.wordpress.com/2014/04/30/zaine-ridling-bible-atlas-e-book/. Use Map 53a, "The United Monarchy," and Map 53, "Kingdom of David and Solomon," to locate key sites mentioned in this section.)

Why did King David leave active service in the Israelite army?

Over the course of time, what nations did David defeat?

What psalm did David write as a prayer for restoration? Read Psalm 60.
Who did David see while walking on his palace roof one evening?

What request did David make? What happened?

Why did David bring Uriah in from the fields of battle?

Why didn't Uriah go home?

What stunt did David pull next to try to accomplish his goal?

When these tactics failed, what terrible thing did David do to Uriah?

What happened to Uriah's wife?
When the Lord sent Nathan to King David, what story did the prophet tell?

What was David's response to Nathan's story?

What was David's response when he realized he was "the rich man"? Read Psalm 51.

> *Discuss possible responses when confronted about sin. Talk about the healing power of God's forgiveness.*

What happened as a result of David's sin?
What city fell to Joab and David?
What other nation came into subjection to David?
What king and city also fell to David?
What people were struck down when they came to help the fallen king?

What nation did Abishai defeat in the Valley of Salt?
What king declared allegiance to David?
What did David do with the tribute and plunder?
Who were "the Three" mighty men?
Who was the commander of "the Three"?

Who was as famous as "the Three" mighty men?

Who was born to David and Bathsheba?
With whom did Amnon fall in love?
What scheme did Jonadab concoct?

What happened when the scheme played out?

What happened when Absalom found out?

What happened when David found out?
How did Absalom get his revenge?

What rumor was told to David?
Who discounted this gossip?

Where did Absalom end up?
How did David feel about Absalom?

Who schemed to get Absalom returned to Jerusalem?
How long was it before David and his son Absalom were reconciled?

Why did Absalom begin to hang out by the city gate?

How long did this go on?
Under what pretense did Absalom request to go to Hebron?

What did Absalom really go to Hebron to do?
What did this action force David to do?
At first, what did David take along?
Who took this important item back to the city? Why?

Who else did David send to spy on Absalom?
What was this spy's mission?

Who came out from Bahurim to curse and throw rocks and dirt at David?

What was his issue with David?

How did David respond to this man?

Why did David write Psalm 3?
What advice did Ahithophel give Absalom about how to attack David?

Who gave different advice?
What was this man's plan of attack?

Whose advice did Absalom accept?
How did David find out about Absalom's plan to attack?

How did Ahithophel react when his advice was not taken?

Who was the commander of Absalom's army?

What did David do to avoid Absalom's attack?

What special request did David ask of his three commanders?

Where did this great battle take place?

Who won?
How many casualties were there?

What happened to Absalom?

How did David find out about Absalom's death?
What was David's reaction to the news?
Why was David's reaction troubling for Joab?

Who did David select as the commander of his army in place of Joab?

As David was returning to Jerusalem as king, who hurried to the Jordan River to meet him?

What did they want?
What did they get?
Who led a rebellion of the men of Israel against David?

Who stayed with David on his journey to Jerusalem?
Who did David send after the guy who was stirring up trouble?

What happened at the great rock in Gibeon?

What action saved the city of Abel Beth Maacah?

When David was reinstated as king in Jerusalem, whom did he appoint as his officials?

What major calamity struck Israel?
Why did this happen?

How did David avenge this wrong?

Where were the bones of Saul, Jonathan, and these men buried?

Who incited David to commit an act that was evil in the sight of the Lord?

What did David do?
Who advised David not to do this?
Who was not included? Why?
What did the Lord think of this?
When David begged for forgiveness, what did the Lord do?

What was David's choice? Why?

How many died before the Lord relented?
What did David do to encourage the Lord to relent?

Even though Araunah offered to give David what he needed, why did David insist on paying full price?

Where was the Lord's tabernacle and altar at this time?
What site was chosen for the new temple?

What preparations did David make for building the temple?

Why was David not allowed to actually build the temple?

Who was given the task of building the temple?
Why was this man chosen?

What advice did David give his son on how to be successful?

What psalm did David write as a song of dedication to the temple? Read Psalm 30.
Before he died, what extensive appointments did David make in order to provide a smooth transition for the next king?

How did the Levites' duties change after the temple was built?

When David convened the great assembly of officials and soldiers, whom did he present as the next king of Israel?

What admonition did David give to this next king?

What did David deliver to the new king?

What did David solicit from the whole assembly?

How did this assembly close?

PSALMS

For a Troubled Soul

Psalm 5–7, 10, 11, 13, 17, 23, 26, 28, 31, 35, 41, 43, 46, 55, 61, 62, 64, 69–71, 77, 83, 86, 88, 91, 95, 108, 109, 120, 121, 140, 143, and 144

Many gospel songs and hymns are based on the Psalms. Match them up as you read through this section. Also, be sure to make a note of your favorites.

List some of the authors of these psalms.

As you read, make a list of the message found in each psalm. Discuss common themes and purposes.

Righteousness vs. Wickedness
Psalm 1, 14, 15, 36, 37, 39, 40, 49, 50, 73, 76, 82, 84, 90, 92, 112, and 115

Make a list of the messages presented in these songs. Discuss common themes.

Joy and Praise
Psalm 8, 9, 16, 19, 21, 24, 29, 33, 65–68, 75, 93, 94, 97–100, 103, 104, 113, 114, 117, 119, 122, 124, 133–136, 138, 139, 145, 148, and 150

Make a list of the messages found in these songs. Discuss common exhortations.

Various Themes
Psalm 4, 12, 20, 25, 32, 38, 42, 53, 58, 81, 101, 111, 130, 131, 141, and 146

Make a list of the heartfelt sentiments being expressed by these authors.

Can you relate to any of these? Which ones? Why?

Messianic
Psalm 2, 22, 27, 45, 47, 48, 87, and 110

What is the central theme of each of these psalms?

Make a list of some of the messianic prophecies presented in these psalms.

Look at your list of modern-day spiritual songs inspired by the Psalms. Think about the messages and themes found in some of today's hymns and gospel songs that are not found in the Psalms.

KING SOLOMON
(971–931 BC)
1 Kings 1:1–10:13, 2 Chronicles 1:2–9:27
Psalm 72

In many ways, Solomon was the greatest man who ever lived. As you read this section, look for character traits that support this statement.

As David's health failed, how was he kept warm?

Who attempted to take the throne?
Whose support did this man have?

Who did not support him?

Who told David about the plot for this other son to become the next king?

What was David's response?

How did the other son react when he heard all the rejoicing?

How did the new king respond?
What were David's last words of advice to his son, the new king of all Israel? (2 Samuel 23: 1-7)

Discuss the significance of David's last words.

What last requests did David make?

Where was David buried?
Why was Adonijah executed?

How did Solomon deal with Abiathar, the priest?

How did this action fulfill the word of the Lord?

Why was Joab executed?

Who did Solomon appoint as his army commander?
Who served as high priest?
What restriction was placed on Shimei?

What would happen if this condition was violated?
What prompted Shimei to violate this restriction?

What was the result of Shimei's action?
What effect did Solomon's judicial decisions have on his leadership position?

Why did Solomon marry Pharaoh's daughter?
What was the Pharaoh's wedding gift to Solomon?

When Solomon went to worship the Lord in the Tent of Meeting at Gibeon, what happened to him?

Discuss how you would respond if given such an opportunity.

What request did young King Solomon make?

Why did God grant Solomon's request?

What did God give Solomon?

Once he returned to Jerusalem, what dispute did Solomon have to settle?

How did Solomon determine the infant's fate?

What effect did this case have on Solomon's judicial reputation?

(Go to https://en.wikipedia.org/wiki/Temple_in_Jerusalem to view images of Solomon's temple and to see some of the temple furnishings. Use these images to help you get a picture of this extravagant building project.)

What two structures did Solomon begin to build?
Why was the timing right for these building projects?

What kind of structure did Solomon intend to build?

What king was enlisted to help?

What materials and services did this king supply? What did he receive in return?

How were the logs to be transported from Lebanon to Jerusalem?

How many laborers were drafted to work in Lebanon?

Who was put in charge of this labor force?
How many foreigners did Solomon assign to work this project?

When did this building project begin?

Where was the chosen building site?

Describe the dimensions of this structure.

Describe the main hall.

What wood was used inside?
Describe the porch.

How many stories were in the structure around the building?

Describe the Most Holy Place.

What sectioned off the Most Holy Place from the rest of the temple?

Describe the entrance doors to the inner sanctuary and main hall?

When was construction completed? How long did it take to complete the temple?

What bronze (brass) work did Hiram (Huram) the artisan complete?

What held up the sea?

What was the purpose of the sea?

How much water did the sea hold?
Describe the stands.

What was the purpose of the bronze basins on the stands?

What other temple articles did Hiram make?
What temple furnishings were made of gold?

What kinds of worship activities took place in the temple?

What did the Levites bring to Jerusalem?

What was in the ark now?

Describe how the Levites and priests gave praises and thanks to the Lord.

What happened during this praise service?

List the main points of Solomon's dedication address.

List some key messages found in Solomon's prayer.

What happened when Solomon finished his prayer and blessed the whole assembly of Israel?

How many animals were sacrificed during the temple dedication and festival celebration?

(Go to https://theologue.wordpress.com/2014/04/30/zaine-ridling-bible-atlas-e-book/. Look at Map 54, "Solomon's Economic Enterprises," and Map 55, "Solomon's Building Activities," to locate sites and activities mentioned in this section.)

How long did it take to build Solomon's palace?
Describe the dimensions of Solomon's palace.

What happened to Solomon when the temple and palace buildings were completed?

What was the message for the Israelites?

What was the message for Solomon?

Who made up the labor force that built the cities?
Where did Pharaoh's daughter (Solomon's wife) live?

In partnership with Hiram, what trade did Solomon start?

(Go to https://theologue.wordpress.com/2014/04/30/zaine-ridling-bible-atlas-e-book/. Look back at Map 53a, "The United Monarchy," and Map 53, "Kingdom of David and Solomon," to locate key sites mentioned in this section.)

How wise was Solomon?

Make a list of all the subjects Solomon knew.

How rich was Solomon?

Describe the extent of Solomon's stables.

Describe the boundaries of Solomon's kingdom.

What was the role of the twelve district governors?

What special visitor came to Jerusalem to test Solomon's wisdom?

What was her impression of Solomon?

What song did Solomon write in celebration of his blessings?

Solomon's Proverbs

As you read through these wise sayings, take note of your favorites. Look for modern-day sayings based on the Proverbs. Also, think about how these teachings cannot only influence an individual's life but can also have a tremendous impact on society as a whole.

What is a proverb?

Who wrote most of Proverbs?

Read the following that pertain to wisdom.
Proverbs 1:1–7 and 20–33
Proverbs 2:1–22
Proverbs 3:13–24
Proverbs 4:1–27
Proverbs 8:1–9:6
Proverbs 9:13–18
Proverbs 22:17–21
According to the writers of these proverbs, who is the source of "wisdom"?

Make a list of some of the characteristics of wisdom.

How many of these characteristics do you possess? Which ones need work?

List some of the benefits of wisdom.

What are some of the dangers faced if wisdom is rejected?

What was Solomon's personal plea regarding wisdom?

What did Solomon say was the value of wise sayings?

What did Solomon say were the purposes of these wise sayings?

What did Solomon say was at the root of all knowledge?

Read the following about the importance of having a respectful fear of the Lord.
Proverbs 9:10–12
Proverbs 10:27
Proverbs 14:2 and 26–27
Proverbs 15:33
Proverbs 19:23
Proverbs 28:14

List the benefits of living in awe of the power of Almighty God.

Read the following about trust.
Proverbs 3:5–8
Proverbs 14:12
Proverbs 16:3, 20, 25
Proverbs 18:2, 4, 10
Proverbs 19:3
Proverbs 20:24
Proverbs 21:22
Proverbs 26:12
Proverbs 28:26
Proverbs 29:25
Where did Solomon say a wise person should put his trust?

Read the following about divine providence.
Proverbs 15:3
Proverbs 16:1, 4, 9, 33
Proverbs 19:21
Proverbs 21:30–31
Proverbs 22:12
Proverbs 27:1
Who did Solomon say was really in charge?

Discuss how God's control over the world is manifested.

Read the following about wisdom and foolishness, including Solomon's advice on how to respond to imparted wisdom.

Proverbs 13:14	Proverbs 10:13, 23	Proverbs 10:14	Proverbs 3:1–2	Proverbs 11:14
Proverbs 14:24	Proverbs 13:15	Proverbs 13:16	Proverbs 9:7–9	Proverbs 15: 22
Proverbs 15:24	Proverbs 14:6, 8, 15, 33	Proverbs 14:18	Proverbs 10:8	Proverbs 20:18
Proverbs 16:22	Proverbs 15:21	Proverbs 15:14	Proverbs 12:15	Proverbs 24:5–6
Proverbs 17:12	Proverbs 16:16	Proverbs 18:15	Proverbs 13:1, 13	
Proverbs 24:7, 13–14	Proverbs 17:24	Proverbs 19:2	Proverbs 15:31	
Proverbs 26:4–11	Proverbs 19:8	Proverbs 20:15	Proverbs 17:10	
Proverbs 27:22	Proverbs 20:5, 12	Proverbs 21:11	Proverbs 19:16, 20, 25, 27	
Proverbs 29:9		Proverbs 23:12	Proverbs 23:9	
		Proverbs 24:3–4	Proverbs 25:12	
			Proverbs 27:5–6, 17	
			Proverbs 29:1	

What advice did Solomon give about how to deal with fools?

What advice did Solomon give about correcting others?

Discuss how this advice might be applied in your own life.

Read the following that deal with discipline.
Proverbs 3:11–12
Proverbs 10:17
Proverbs 12:1
Proverbs 13:18, 24
Proverbs 15:5, 10, 12, 32
Proverbs 19:18
Proverbs 20:30
Proverbs 22:6, 15
Proverbs 23:13–14
Proverbs 28:4, 7, 9
Proverbs 29:15, 17–19, 21
Why did Solomon say discipline was so important?

Read the following that discuss good and evil.

Proverbs 10:6–7, 16, 28–30   Proverbs 20:7

Proverbs 11:5–10, 18–20, 23   Proverbs 21:18

Proverbs 12:2–3, 5–8, 12, 21, 28   Proverbs 24:15–16

Proverbs 13:9, 21, 25   Proverbs 28:12, 28

Proverbs 14:11, 19, 34   Proverbs 29:2, 16, 27   Proverbs 15:6, 9

Compare and contrast good versus evil.

Read the following that discuss integrity vs. perversion, and describe the consequences of one's choices.

Proverbs 10:9   Proverbs 3:33–35

Proverbs 13:6   Proverbs 10:3, 22, 24–25

Proverbs 15:26   Proverbs 11:21, 27, 30–31

Proverbs 21:8   Proverbs 14:14, 22

Proverbs 24:8–9   Proverbs 16:7

Proverbs 28:18   Proverbs 17:13

Proverbs 29:10   Proverbs 18:3

Proverbs 19:29

Proverbs 21:12, 16, 21

Proverbs 22:8

Proverbs 26:1, 3, 27

Compare and contrast the characteristics of a life of integrity versus a life of perversion.

Make a list of some predictable consequences of wicked behavior.

What did Solomon say would be found if righteousness and love were pursued?

Read the following about the importance of having a sincere heart.

Proverbs 15:11	Proverbs 15:8, 29	Proverbs 6:12–15
Proverbs 16:2	Proverbs 21:3, 27	Proverbs 10:10–11
Proverbs 17:3		Proverbs 11:3
Proverbs 20:11, 27		Proverbs 16:30
Proverbs 21:2		Proverbs 20:14
Proverbs 27:19		Proverbs 23:6–8
Proverbs 26:23–26		

What did Solomon say was tested by the Lord? Why?

Read the following that deal with love and the treatment of others.

Proverbs 3:3–4	Proverbs 10:12	Proverbs 11:16–17
Proverbs 16:6	Proverbs 15:17	Proverbs 12:10, 25
Proverbs 20:6	Proverbs 17:5	Proverbs 21:10
Proverbs 25:19	Proverbs 24:17–18	
	Proverbs 25:21–22	

How did Solomon describe love and faithfulness?

What effect did Solomon say a kind word had on an anxious heart?
Read the following that deal with pride, humility, selfishness, jealousy, envy, and greed.

Proverbs 11:2	Proverbs 18:1	Proverbs 14:30
Proverbs 12:9	Proverbs 27:4	Proverbs 24:19–20
Proverbs 13:7, 10		Proverbs 28:25
Proverbs 15:25		
Proverbs 16:5, 18–19		
Proverbs 18:12		
Proverbs 19:10		
Proverbs 20:9		
Proverbs 21:4, 24		
Proverbs 22:4		
Proverbs 25:27		
Proverbs 26:16		
Proverbs 27:2, 21		
Proverbs 29:23		

Compare and contrast pride versus humility.

Contrast the effect of envy on the body versus a heart at peace?

Read the following that deal with self-control.

Proverbs 25:28	Proverbs 20:25	Proverbs 12:16	Proverbs 20:1
Proverbs 29:11	Proverbs 25:8	Proverbs 14:16–17, 29	Proverbs 23:19–21, 29–35
	Proverbs 29:20	Proverbs 15:18	
	Proverbs 16:32	Proverbs 5:1–23	
	Proverbs 19:11, 19	Proverbs 6:20–35	
	Proverbs 22:24–25	Proverbs 7:1–27	
	Proverbs 29:8, 22	Proverbs 22:14	

List the characteristics of someone who does *not* demonstrate self-control.

List some characteristics of a person who eats and drinks too much.

What advice did Solomon give concerning adultery?

Read the following that give advice on watching what you say. (Notice how many verses deal with this topic.)

Proverbs 14:3	Proverbs 10:20–21, 31–32	Proverbs 15:23	Proverbs 10:19
Proverbs 15:2, 7	Proverbs 11:11	Proverbs 16:21, 24	Proverbs 12:23
Proverbs 16:23	Proverbs 12:13–14	Proverbs 25:11	Proverbs 13:3
Proverbs 18:6–7	Proverbs 13:2	Proverbs 27:14	Proverbs 17:28
Proverbs 19:1	Proverbs 15:28	Proverbs 18:13	
Proverbs 23:15–16	Proverbs 17:4	Proverbs 21:23	
Proverbs 15:1	Proverbs 10:18	Proverbs 20:19	Proverbs 11:12
Proverbs 17:27	Proverbs 11:13	Proverbs 26:20	Proverbs 12:18
Proverbs 25:15	Proverbs 16:28	Proverbs 15:4	
Proverbs 26:28	Proverbs 17:9	Proverbs 16:27	
Proverbs 28:23	Proverbs 18:8	Proverbs 25:23	
Proverbs 29:5		Proverbs 26:22	Proverbs 26:2
Proverbs 17:14, 19	Proverbs 12:19, 22	Proverbs 18:20–21	

Proverbs 20:3   Proverbs 17:20
Proverbs 22:10   Proverbs 19:5, 22
Proverbs 26:21   Proverbs 21:6

Contrast wise versus foolish/wicked talk.

List some characteristics of godly talk.

Why do you think Solomon gave so much advice on this topic?

Read the following with advice on how to avoid a life of disharmony and trouble.

Proverbs 1:10–19   Proverbs 3:29–32   Proverbs 20:22   Proverbs 6:16–19
Proverbs 16:29   Proverbs 21:7, 29   Proverbs 24:28–29   Proverbs 17:1
Proverbs 25:26   Proverbs 28:17   Proverbs 18:18–19
Proverbs 27:3   Proverbs 26:17
Proverbs 28:10

List some behaviors that lead to disharmony and trouble.

List six things the Lord hates.

Why do you think the Lord hates these things?

Read the following that deal with the importance of being honest and just.

Proverbs 12:20   Proverbs 11:1   Proverbs 10:2   Proverbs 15:27
Proverbs 13:5   Proverbs 16:11   Proverbs 13:11   Proverbs 17:8, 23
Proverbs 24:26   Proverbs 20:10, 23   Proverbs 20:17, 21   Proverbs 21:14
Proverbs 26:18–19 Proverbs 22:28
                  Proverbs 23:10–11
Proverbs 12:17   Proverbs 17:15, 26

Proverbs 14:5, 25	Proverbs 18:5
Proverbs 19:9, 28	Proverbs 21:15
Proverbs 21:28	Proverbs 24:11–12, 23–25
Proverbs 25:18	Proverbs 28:5
	Proverbs 29:26

List some characteristics of honesty.
Describe justice.

Read the following that deal with wealth and poverty.

Proverbs 3:9–10	Proverbs 3:27–28	Proverbs 13:23	Proverbs 6:6–11
Proverbs 10:15	Proverbs 11:24–26	Proverbs 14:31	Proverbs 10:4–5, 26
Proverbs 11:4, 28	Proverbs 13:22	Proverbs 15:15	Proverbs 12:11, 24, 27
Proverbs 13:8	Proverbs 14:21	Proverbs 16:8	Proverbs 13:4
Proverbs 14:20	Proverbs 18:16	Proverbs 22:16, 22–23	Proverbs 14:4, 23
Proverbs 15:16	Proverbs 19:17	Proverbs 29:7, 13	Proverbs 15:19
Proverbs 17:16	Proverbs 21:13	Proverbs 16:26	
Proverbs 18:11, 23	Proverbs 22:9	Proverbs 20:4, 13	Proverbs 18:9
Proverbs 19:4, 6	Proverbs 25:14	Proverbs 21:17, 25–26	Proverbs 19:15, 24
Proverbs 22:2, 7	Proverbs 28:27	Proverbs 22:29	Proverbs 26:15
Proverbs 23:4–5	Proverbs 24:27, 30–34		
Proverbs 27:7	Proverbs 26:14	Proverbs 21:20	
Proverbs 28:6, 8, 11, 20–22	Proverbs 27:18, 23–27		
	Proverbs 28:19		

How did Solomon say wealth should be viewed?

List some characteristics of a lazy person and of laziness.

Read the following that give relationship advice.

Proverbs 1:8–9	Proverbs 16:31	Proverbs 11:22	Proverbs 14:28, 35
Proverbs 10:1	Proverbs 20:29	Proverbs 12:4	Proverbs 16:10, 12–15
Proverbs 11:29		Proverbs 14:1	Proverbs 17:7, 11
Proverbs 15:20		Proverbs 18:22	Proverbs 19:12
Proverbs 17:2, 6, 21, 25	Proverbs 19:13–14	Proverbs 20:2, 8, 26, 28	
Proverbs 19:26		Proverbs 21:9, 19	Proverbs 21:1
Proverbs 20:20		Proverbs 25:24	Proverbs 22:11
Proverbs 23:22–25		Proverbs 27:15–16	Proverbs 23:1–3
Proverbs 28:24			Proverbs 24:21–22
			Proverbs 25:2–7
Proverbs 12:26			Proverbs 28:2–3, 15–16
Proverbs 13:20			Proverbs 29:4, 12, 14
Proverbs 14:7			
Proverbs 17:17			
Proverbs 18:24			
Proverbs 24:1–2			
Proverbs 27: 8–10			
Proverbs 29:24			

What instruction did Solomon give to parents and children?

List some characteristics of a good king.

Why did Solomon say it was so important to choose good friends?

> *Discuss the qualities that make a person a "good" friend. How many of these qualities do you possess? Which ones need work?*

Read the following that give advice on the importance of being careful, guarding your reputation, and having courage and hope.

Proverbs 16:17   Proverbs 22:1   Proverbs 3:25–26   Proverbs 13:12, 19
Proverbs 22:3, 5   Proverbs 25:9–10   Proverbs 14:32   Proverbs 23:17–18
Proverbs 27:12   Proverbs 22:13
                                        Proverbs 24:10
                                        Proverbs 26:13
                                        Proverbs 28:1

Why was Solomon so concerned about being careful? Having a good reputation? Having courage? Having hope?

Discuss some practical applications of these wise teachings.

Read Proverbs 30.
Who was Agur?

What two things did Agur request?

What four things did Agur say never seem to be satisfied?

What four things did Agur say were so amazing he could not understand them?

What four things did Agur say the earth could not withstand?

What four things did Agur say were small but wise?

What four things did Agur say moved with a stately purpose?

Read Proverbs 31:1–9.
Who was King Lemuel?
What advice did King Lemuel give?

Read Proverbs 31:10–31.
List the characteristics of a noble wife.

Solomon's Song of Songs
Psalm 127; Song of Songs 1:1–8:14

What message do you think Solomon was trying to convey when he wrote Psalm 127?

How would you describe Solomon's Song of Songs?

Solomon's Ecclesiastes
1 Kings 11:1–40; Ecclesiastes 1:1–12:14

As you read through this section take note of the humanity found in the great King Solomon and immerse yourself in his answer to the question, "What is the meaning of life?"

What caused Solomon to sin?

What effect did this sin have on Solomon?

How did Solomon's actions affect his relationship with God?

Who was chosen to cause problems for Solomon and Israel?

What did the prophet Ahijah tell Jeroboam?

What did Solomon try to do to Jeroboam?

What did the Teacher say was the ultimate question?

What common fate will be shared by animals/man, foolish/wise, righteous/wicked, and hard workers/idle?

How did the Teacher describe himself?

How did he define "all the things that are done" by men?

What did he have to say about laughter and pleasure?
How did he feel about the result of doing great things?

What life conditions did the Teacher describe as being "empty"?

What did the Teacher say was a "gift from God"?

Why did the Teacher say wisdom was valuable?

The Teacher said there was a time for everything. Make a list contrasting these.

Why did the Teacher say God made everything beautiful and set the concept of eternity in the hearts of men?

What advice did the Teacher give to young people?

Discuss the impact this advice can have on your life.

What did the Teacher say was the meaning of life?

Solomon's Death
(931 BC)
1 Kings 11:41–43; 2 Chronicles 9:29–31

How long did Solomon reign in Jerusalem over all Israel?

Where was he buried?

Who succeeded Solomon as king?

(Go to https://theologue.wordpress.com/2014/04/30/zaine-ridling-bible-atlas-e-book/. Look at Map 57, "The Kingdoms of Israel and Judah," and track the new boundaries established by the split of the Promised Land.)

Israel Divided

(930–725 BC)

As you read this section, continue to complete the chart of the kings of Israel and Judah. Also, look for decisions and consequences that led to the total breakdown of God's relationship with His people.

ISRAEL AND JUDAH
(931 BC)
1 Kings 12:1–16:34; 2 Chronicles 10:1–18:1;
I Kings 22: 41-47; 2 Chronicles 20: 31-33

Who was the new king of Israel?
What was the first problem he faced?

Whose advice did he seek? What was the advice?

What decision did the new king make?

> *Think about a time when you listened to your friends instead of your elders. What were the consequences?*

Why did this happen?
Describe the consequences of this decision.

Why did Jeroboam set up altars to idols at Dan and Bethel?

Why did the Levites and those faithful to God flee to Judah?

How long were they faithful?
What prophecy was delivered to Jeroboam at the altar at Bethel?

How did Jeroboam know this prophecy came from the Lord?

What command had the Lord given to the prophet from Judah?

Who gave the prophet from Judah conflicting information?

What happened to the prophet from Judah?
What prompted Jeroboam's wife to disguise herself and go to Shiloh?

Even though he was blind, how did Ahijah know who the woman really was?

What was the Lord's message?

Where did Rehoboam go wrong?

What happened in the fifth year of Rehoboam's reign?

Why did the Lord allow this to happen?

Why was Judah not totally destroyed?

Describe the current relationship between Israel and Judah.
How old was Rehoboam when he became king?
How long did he reign?
Who succeeded Rehoboam as king of Judah?
How long did he reign over Judah?
How was this new king of Judah able to survive Jeroboam's ambush and win the war in Ephraim?

Describe the character of this king of Judah.

Who was the next king of Judah?
Describe his character.

How long was Jeroboam king of Israel?
Who succeeded Jeroboam as king of Israel?
How long did this new king reign over Israel?
Describe his character.
How did his reign end?
Who was the next king of Israel?

How did this king of Israel treat Jeroboam's family?

How long did this king reign over Israel?

Describe his character.
Who attacked Asa and the army of Judah at Mareshah?
Who won this battle? Why?

What warning did the prophet Azariah give to Asa?

How did Asa respond to Azariah's message?

Who did Asa go to for help in the fight against Israel?
Why did Hanani the seer rebuke Asa?

What were the consequences of Asa's actions?

What warning did the prophet Jehu give Baasha?

Who became the next king of Israel?
How long did he reign over Israel?
What happened to this king?

Who was the next king of Israel?
How long did he rule?
What was this king's first official action?

How did his reign end?

Who was the next king of Israel?
What happened after four years of his rule?
How long did he rule Israel alone?
What city did this king build as the new capital of Israel?
Describe the character of this king.
Who was the next king of Israel?
How long did he rule Israel?
Describe the character of this king.

What important city was rebuilt during this time?

How long did Asa rule as king of Judah?
Who succeeded Asa as king of Judah?
How old was he?
How long did he rule Judah?

Describe the character of this king of Judah.

(Go to https://theologue.wordpress.com/2014/04/30/zaine-ridling-bible-atlas-e-book/. Look at Map 62, "Elijah and Elisha.")

PROPHETS OF ISRAEL AND JUDAH

Name	*Dates (B.C.)	King(s) at the Time	Main Message
Elijah			
Elisha			
Obadiah?			
Joel?			
Jonah			
Hosea			
Amos			
Micah			
Isaiah			
Nahum			
Zephaniah			
Jeremiah			
Habakkuk			
Daniel			
Ezekiel			

*Dates taken from Rose Book of Bible Charts, Maps & Time Lines, Rose Publishing, 2005, pgs. 64-65 and from NIV
Life Application Study Bible, Tyndale House Publishers, Inc. and Zondervan Publishers, 2011, pgs. 578-579.

PROPHETS AND PROPHECIES

> *As you read this section, continue to complete the chart of the kings and fill in the chart of the prophets of Israel and Judah. Look for examples of how faithfulness to God is rewarded and how disobedience is punished.*

Elijah
1 Kings 17:1–22:49; 2 Chronicles 18:2–20:37
2 Kings 1:1–18, 3:1–3

Who was a powerful prophet during Ahab's reign?
What catastrophic event did this prophet predict?

While this prophet was hiding out in the Kerith Ravine, how was he able to get food and water?

When the Lord sent him to Zarephath, how was he able to eat?

What miracle did this prophet perform while staying with a widow?

What was the result of this miracle?

How long had the drought lasted?
Who did Ahab summon to try to find some grazing for his animals?

How had this man protected God's prophets?

What did Elijah request from this man?

Why was this request a dangerous one?

Describe the historical confrontation that took place.

What were the odds?
What was the test?

What was the outcome?

What action did Elijah take?

What was the Lord's response?

How did the people respond?

How did Jezebel respond?
What was Elijah's response?

How did God reassure Elijah?

Where wasn't the Lord?
Where was the Lord?
What was the Lord's message to Elijah?

Ahab and Jezebel
(857 BC)

Who attacked Ahab and Israel in Samaria?

Who gave Ahab and Israel the victory? Why?

What happened the following spring?

What was the outcome?

Whose life did Ahab spare?

What was the consequence of Ahab's decision?

How long was there peace between Israel and Aram (Syria)?
What property did Ahab covet?

How did Jezebel scheme to get this land for Ahab?

What punishment did Elijah prophesy for Ahab?

How did Ahab delay this punishment?

Who was named as king along with Ahab?
How long did he rule over Israel?
Name the two kings who joined forces to take Ramoth Gilead back from Aram (Syria).

What prophecy was given concerning this upcoming battle?

What was Micaiah's prophecy?

Why didn't Ahab want to listen to what Micaiah had to say?

What happened to Ahab during the battle for Ramoth Gilead?

What did Jehu the seer have to say to the king of Judah when the king returned to Jerusalem?

Describe the character of this current king of Israel.

After Ahab's death, who rebelled against Israel?
When faced with invasion by the Moabites, what did the people of Judah do?

What was God's answer?

What was the outcome of the battle with the Moabites?

What was the result of this triumph?

What alliance did Jehoshaphat make with Ahaziah?

What was the result of this pact?

What did Elijah predict would happen to Ahaziah after he fell from an upper window and injured himself?
What was Ahaziah's response to this prophecy?

What happened when these men found Elijah?

What happened when Elijah confronted Ahaziah?

Who became the next king of Israel?

How long did this man rule Israel?
Describe the character of this king.

Elisha
2 Kings 2:1–2:25, 4:1–44, 8:1–2, 6:1–7, 22:45, 50, 8:18–22
2 Chronicles 20: 34, 21: 1 - 20

Who was with Elijah during his last days?

What message did the company of prophets at Bethel and Jericho have for Elisha?

What miracle did Elijah perform when he and Elisha reached the Jordan River?

What gift did Elisha request from Elijah?
Describe how Elijah left this earth.

What miracle did Elisha perform at the Jordan River?

What was the result of this miracle?

What miracle did Elisha perform at Jericho?

What was Elisha's response when some kids from Bethel made fun of him?

How did Elisha help the prophet's widow?

Who provided Elisha food and a place to stay when he was in Shunem?

What did Elisha do to reward this woman for her generosity?

What miracles did Elisha perform during the famine in Gilgal?

Why did the Shunammite woman travel all the way to Mount Carmel?

What was Elisha's response?

Why did the woman and her son go to the land of the Philistines?

What additional miracle did Elisha perform at the Jordan River?

Who was named as king of Judah along with Jehoshaphat?

What was his first official action as co-ruler?

Name the three kings who joined forces to fight against Moab.

What tactical mistake did these kings make?

Who did the kings go to for help?
Describe what happened and explain why.

What optical illusion led to the Moabites' defeat?

Describe the character of the reigning king of Judah.

What was so mysterious about a letter received by the king?

What was this letter's message?

What happened to the land of Judah as a result of this king forsaking the Lord, the God of his fathers?

Obadiah
The Book of Obadiah; 2 Chronicles 21:18–24:2
2 Kings 5:1–27 6:8–7:20, 8:3–12:3

What does the name "Obadiah" mean?
Who was he?
Briefly describe who the Edomites were and explain their history with the Israelites.

What rebuke from the Lord did Obadiah have for Edom?

What was to be the fate of the Edomites?

Why was this going to happen?

What happened to King Jehoram?

Why did the king of Aram (Syria) think he had a spy in his camp?

How was Elisha able to avoid capture?

Who returned from the land of the Philistines? Why?

What did this woman want?

What was the resolution of her case?

Who was Naaman?

Who gave Naaman medical advice?

What was this advice?
How did Naaman respond to this advice?

What "cure" was Naaman given?

How did Naaman respond to this advice?

Who else gave Naaman advice?
What was this advice?

> *Think about a time in your life when God asked you to do a "little" thing. How did you respond?*

How did Naaman respond to this advice?

What was the result of this miracle?

What sin did Elisha's servant commit?

What was Gehazi's punishment?

What happened when Ben-Hadad, the king of Syria, laid siege to Samaria?

Who did the king of Israel blame?
What was the result of this king's lack of faith?

What happened to the Syrian forces that were holding the city?

Who made the discovery?

Who thought this information was a trap?
What happened to this man?

How did the people feel about the death of King Jehoram?

Who succeeded Jehoram as king of Judah?
How old was he?
How long did he reign?
Describe the character of this young king.

What prophecy did Elisha give to Hazael, servant to Ben-Hadad?

How did the king's servant respond to this message?

Which two kings joined forces against the Arameans (Syrians) at Ramoth Gilead?

When one king left the battlefield to go to Jezreel to check on the other king who was wounded, who did Elisha have anointed as the next king of Israel?

How did the lookout know who was approaching Jezreel?

What happened to the reigning king of Israel?

What happened to the reigning king of Judah?

What happened to Jezebel?

What happened to the seventy sons (princes) of Ahab?

What happened to the relatives of Ahaziah, king of Judah?
What happened to Ahaziah, king of Judah?

Who joined Jehu's mission for the Lord?
What did Athaliah do when her son, King Ahaziah of Judah, was killed by Jehu?

How was one prince able to escape?

Under what pretense did Jehu lure all Baal's prophets to the temple of Baal?

What happened to Baal's prophets?

Where did Jehu stop short?

Who did the priest Jehoiada anoint as the next king of Judah?
What happened to Queen Athaliah?

How long did this child-king reign in Jerusalem over Judah?
What other changes did Jehoiada make?
As the main advisor to the king, where did Jehoiada stop short?

Joel

The Book of Joel; 2 Chronicles 24:3–27
2 Kings 10:32–36, 12:4–13:20

What invasion did the prophet Joel describe?

What comparison did Joel make to another kind of invasion?

How did Joel say this tragedy could be avoided?

What event did Joel prophesy?

How did Joel say the people should prepare for this event?

How did Joel say the Lord would respond?

Was Joel talking about Judah at that time or God's people at judgment day?
What order did King Joash give to the Levites?

How did the Levites respond?
How did the Lord reduce the size of Israel?

How long did Jehu rule Israel from Samaria?
Who succeeded him as king of Israel?
How long did this king reign over Israel?
Describe the character of this king.
Explain how the money needed for temple repairs was finally collected.

How old was Jehoiada when he died?
Where was he buried?
What happened to Joash after Jehoiada died?

Who was the priest after Jehoiada?
What happened to this priest?

What effect did Syrian oppression have on the king of Israel?

How did the Lord punish Judah for her disobedience?

Explain how this invasion was finally stopped.

Who succeeded Jehoahaz as king of Israel?
How long did he reign in Samaria?
Describe the character of this king.

What was Elisha's deathbed prophecy?

What happened to Joash, the king of Judah?

(Go to https://theologue.wordpress.com/2014/04/30/zaine-ridling-bible-atlas-e-book/. Use Map 65, "Israel and Judah in the Days of Jeroboam II and Uzziah," to track events that occurred during this time.)

Who succeeded Joash as king of Judah?
How old was he?
How long did he reign in Jerusalem over Judah?
Describe the character of this king of Judah.

Once the kingdom was firmly in his grasp, what did this king do?

What happened when Moabite raiders surprised an Israelite burial party?

Why didn't God give up on the Israelites?

Describe how Elisha's deathbed prophecy came true.

Who did King Amaziah and Judah plan to attack?
Who did they hire to help in this fight?
Why were these troops sent home before the battle?

How did these troops respond after they were dismissed?

What mistake did King Amaziah make when he returned from the battlefield?

What was the result of his error in judgment?

Who succeeded Jehoash as the king of Israel?
How long did he reign as king of Israel?
Describe the character of this king.

Jonah

(780–775 BC)

The Book of Jonah; 2 Kings 13:5–6, 14:25–27

Where did God want Jonah to go? Why?

How did Jonah respond?

> *Discussion: Has there ever been a time in your life when God asked you to do something and you responded like Jonah?*

What happened after the ship set sail?

Describe how those on board solved this dangerous situation.

How did God take care of Jonah?

How long was Jonah in this place?
What did Jonah do during this time?
What was the Lord's response?
What was Jonah's response to God's request the second time?
Describe the response of the Ninevites.

How did God respond?

What was Jonah's reaction to the Ninevites' repentance?

How did God teach Jonah a very important lesson?

> *Discussion: What important lesson did God teach you during your Jonah experience?*

To what other nation did Jonah carry the word of God?
Describe the result.

Hosea
The Book of Hosea; 2 Kings 14:17–22, 15:1–4; 2 Chronicles 25:25–26:15

Name the kings of Judah and Israel who reigned during the time of the prophet Hosea.

What did the Lord ask Hosea to do to exemplify His message and warn the people of Israel?

What was the name of Hosea's wife?
Explain the significance of the name chosen for Hosea's firstborn son.

Explain the meaning of the name chosen for Hosea's daughter.

Explain the meaning of the name chosen for Hosea's second son.

What was Hosea's prophecy about the future of God's people?

How did Hosea feel about his wife's sins? What did Hosea want to do?

What did Hosea do instead?

Explain how Hosea's life was an analogy for God's relationship with Israel.

What charge did Hosea make against Israel?

Describe the consequences of Israel's sins.

What did Hosea say Israel's response would be?

How did Hosea say this relationship would turn out?

What would Israel's punishment be for her unfaithfulness to God?

In spite of Israel's sins, how did God feel about this nation?

Discuss how unfaithfulness to God is still played out like the events of Hosea's life even today.

What happened to King Amaziah of Judah?

Who succeeded him as king of Judah?
How old was he?
How long did this king rule Judah from Jerusalem?
Describe the character of this young king.

How did God bless this king's faithfulness?

Amos
The Book of Amos; 2 Kings 14:28–29, 15:5, 8–18; 2 Chronicles 26:16–21

Who was Amos?

Who were the kings of Judah and Israel at this time?

What nations were going to be judged by God for their ill treatment of His people?

Describe their punishment.

Why was Judah going to be punished?

Why was Israel going to be punished?

What disasters did God use to warn His people of His displeasure?

What did God's unfaithful people need to do to prepare for judgment day?

Discuss what we need to do today to prepare for God's judgment.

Describe judgment day.

Describe how the Israelites' religious rituals were being performed.

What did Amos prophesy about the fate of Israel?
What attitudes led to Israel's downfall?
What five visions did Amos describe?

What promise did Amos make?

How did Amaziah the priest respond to the prophecies of Amos?

How did Amos respond?

Who succeeded Jeroboam II as king of Israel?
How long did he reign?
Describe his character.
What happened to this short-lived king?

Why did this happen?

How long did this "killer" king rule over Israel?
What happened to him?
How long did this cruel king rule from Samaria?
What sin led to King Uzziah's downfall in Judah?

Since Uzziah's condition made it impossible for him to run the day-to-day affairs of Judah, who ruled with him?

Isaiah

Isaiah 1:1–4:6, 5:8–30
2 Kings 15:6–7, 19–28, 32–35
2 Chronicles 26:22–27:8

> *As you read through this section, look for evidence of God's patience with His people, but also look for signs that enough is enough. Take note of prophecies predicting the fall of Israel, judgment day, the restoration of God's people, and salvation through the Messiah. Continue to complete your charts.*

Who was the king of Judah at this time?

List three prophets of Israel.

Who was the prophet of Judah at this time?

How long did this prophet's ministry last?

List the kings of Judah who reigned during his time.

What condemnation did this prophet give about Judah?

How were the people of Jerusalem compared to a vineyard?

Why were Judah's religious rituals not pleasing to God?

Make a list of Judah's sins. Briefly describe each.

What would be the consequences of Judah's sins?

Who would not be able to save Judah?

What would the Lord have preferred rather than punishment?

Who did King Menahem pay to stay out of Israel?
After the death of Menahem, who became king of Israel?
How long did this king reign?
Describe the character of this king of Israel.
Describe what happened to him.

How long did this king rule Israel?
Describe the character of this king of Israel.
How old was Jotham when he became the sole ruler of Judah after his father Uzziah died?

How long did he reign?
Describe the character of this king of Judah.

Describe Isaiah's vision and mission.

How was Jotham able to grow powerful as the king of Judah?

Micah
The Book of Micah

Who was this prophet of Judah?
Who were the kings of Judah during the time of this prophet?
What was prophesied about Israel?

What would happen to Judah as a result of copying Israel's sin?

Describe the sin of covetousness.

Describe the reward of greed.
Who did this prophet say would be just the right preacher for Judah?

In spite of Judah's sinful situation, what was promised?

What did this prophet have to say about the Israelite leaders?

What did he have to say about false prophets?

How did this prophet describe himself?

What did he prophesy would happen to Jerusalem?

What did he say would happen in "the last days"?

Where was the "Daughter of Zion" going?

What did he say would happen in Bethlehem?

What did this prophet say God really wanted?

Discuss how this applies to us even today.

In spite of Judah's sin, what plan was prophesied?

CAPTIVITY BEGINS
2 Kings 15:29; 2 Chronicles 5:23–26

(Go to https://theologue.wordpress.com/2014/04/30/zaine-ridling-bible-atlas-e-book/. Use Map 68, "Tiglath-Pileser III's Campaigns and Areas Transformed into Assyrian Provinces," and Map 69, "The Fall of Samaria and Deportation of Israelites," to track events as they occurred during this time.)

Who were the first captives taken from Israel?

Who captured them?

SYRIA, ISRAEL, AND JUDAH AT WAR
2 Kings 15:30 – 16: 4, 17: 2; 2 Chronicles 27:7 – 28:4

What two nations threatened Judah?
What happened to the current king of Israel?
Who became the next king of Israel?
How long did he reign?
Describe the character of this king of Israel.
Who succeeded Jotham as king of Judah?
How old was he?

How long did he reign?
Describe the character of this king of Judah.

MORE PROPHECIES FROM ISAIAH

Regarding a Messiah
Isaiah 7:1–12:6; 2 Kings 16:5–6; 2 Chronicles 28:5–21

As Syria and Israel were preparing to attack King Ahaz and Jerusalem, what message did God send through Isaiah?

How did Ahaz respond?
What sign did Isaiah give anyway?

What did Isaiah prophesy about Judah, Israel, and Syria?

During these fearsome times, who was to be trusted?
Who did Isaiah say was coming to enlarge the nation and cause the people to rejoice?

What caused God to be angry at Israel?

Why was God going to punish Assyria?

Who was to be saved and brought back from captivity?

What was Isaiah's prophecy about who was to come from the line of David?

What was the outcome of the battle between Judah and Israel/Syria?

Why were the captives released and not enslaved?

Who did King Ahaz pay to help protect Judah from her enemies?

Against Unfriendly Nations
Isaiah 34:1-17, 14:24-32, 15:1-17:14, 21:11-17, 23:1-18; 2 Kings 16:7-20, 18:1-7;
2 Chronicles 28:22-29:2; Isaiah 13:1-14:32, 21:1-10; 2 Chronicles 29:3-31:21

What was the relationship between Judah and Assyria at this time?

List the foreign nations God used to punish Judah.

If God was using them, why was He still angry with them?

After King Ahaz of Judah paid off Tiglath-Pileser, king of Assyria, what happened to Syria?

What did King Ahaz do to provoke God's anger even more?

Who succeeded Ahaz as king of Judah?
How old was he?
How long did this king rule Judah?
Describe the character of this king.

During the year Ahaz died, what nations did Isaiah say would be judged by God?

What was to happen to Babylon?
To what did Isaiah compare the fall of Babylon?
What changes did King Hezekiah make to bring the people back into a right worship relationship with God?

Why was Hezekiah so successful?

Discuss how this applies to us today.

Regarding the Last Days
Isaiah 24:1–27:1, 32:1–8, 35:1–10, 28:1–29:24, 22:1–25, 32:12–33:24

What did Isaiah say would happen in the "last days"?

What did Isaiah say would happen when the people fell away from God?

What was going to happen to Jerusalem?
What was going to happen to the enemies of God's people?

Why didn't God's people understand Isaiah's prophecies?

What was Isaiah's prophecy about the Israelites return to Jerusalem?

What did Isaiah say would happen to Shebna, the man in charge of the palace?

Who was to be his replacement?

ISRAEL FALLS
(726–723 BC)
2 Kings 17:3–41, 18:7–12

> God has finally had enough, but still loves His people. Look for evidence of this, especially in another flawed king with a good heart.

Who was the current king of Assyria?
Why was he so upset with King Hoshea of Israel?

What happened to King Hoshea and to Samaria?

Why did Israel fall?

Discuss the lessons learned from the fall of Israel.

Which tribe was the only one left?
How was Israel repopulated?

What happened to these people?
How was this situation resolved?

How did this solution work out?

How did the rebellion against Assyria and the battle between the Philistines and Judah turn out for King Hezekiah?

Judah after the Fall of Israel
(725–585 BC)

MORE PROPHECIES FROM ISAIAH
(714–711 BC)
Isaiah 18:1–20:6, 30:1–31:9

What was Isaiah's judgment against Cush?

What was Isaiah's judgment against Egypt?

Why did Isaiah go around without sackcloth and sandals for three years?

What did Judah rely on for military strength and protection?

In whom did Isaiah say Judah should have put her trust?

How would God respond when the people of Zion cried out to Him for help?

What was prophesied about Assyria?

THE END OF HEZEKIAH'S REIGN
(701–696 BC)
2 Kings 18:13–19:36; Isaiah 36:1; 2 Kings 20:1–21:16
2 Chronicles 32:1–33:9; Isaiah 38:1–22, 39:1–8, 36:2–37:37

Who attacked and captured the fortified cities of Judah?

How did King Hezekiah get this enemy to withdraw?

According to Isaiah, what was to be the outcome of King Hezekiah's illness?

What was the king's response to this news?

What was the result of Hezekiah's actions?

What was the Lord's sign that this promise would be fulfilled?

When they heard about Hezekiah's illness, who sent representatives to check the situation out?

What prideful, foolish thing did Hezekiah do when tested by God?

What did Isaiah say would be the result of this error in judgment?

Who was coming back to invade Judah?
Describe the war preparations made by Hezekiah.

What message did Sennacherib's field commander have for Hezekiah and the people of Judah?

How well did this intimidation tactic work?

What did Isaiah predict would happen to this Assyrian field commander as a result of his ridiculing God?

What intimidation tactic did Assyria try next?

What was Hezekiah's reaction?

How did God respond?

How did Hezekiah get water into the city during this attack?
How did the people of Judah react to Hezekiah's death?

Who succeeded Hezekiah as king of Judah?
How old was he? How long did he reign?
Describe the character of this king of Judah.

What did the prophets warn would be the result of this king's actions?

MORE RESTORATION AND MESSIANIC
PROPHECIES FROM ISAIAH
Isaiah 40:1–66:24

As you read through this section, take note of how God and the Messiah are described. Be able to explain how this Messiah will bring about salvation. Continue to complete your charts.

What was Isaiah's prophecy about what would happen after God's punishment was complete?

Why would God do this?

How did Isaiah describe God's strength?

How did Isaiah describe the strength given to man as a result of his relationship with God?

How did Isaiah describe God's relationship with the Israel nation?

Describe the person who Isaiah prophesied would bring justice on earth.

What was God's plan for this person?

What were the consequences for Israel's unwillingness to listen and remain faithful to God?

After their punishment, what was God's plan for Israel?

What did Isaiah prophesy about Babylon?
What would be the new relationship between God and Israel?

What did Isaiah prophesy about Judah and Jerusalem?

Who did God intend to use to make this happen?

What did God demonstrate by the restoration of Israel and the fall of Babylon?

Summarize Isaiah's prophecy about the exile of the Israelites from Judah and their restoration.

How did Isaiah describe the coming Messiah?

What role would He play in the cleansing of sins?

How would He behave when accused and judged?

Discuss what Isaiah meant when he wrote, "After the suffering of his soul, he will see the light of life" (Isaiah 53:11).

List some of the names Isaiah gave to God in his description of Israel as God's wife.

How did Isaiah compare God's way of thinking to man's?

Who did Isaiah say would be saved?

Why did Isaiah say righteous people die?

Who did Isaiah say would not be restored?
What day did Isaiah say should be honored as holy?
What separated the people from God?
When the Redeemer came to Zion, who would be saved?
How did Isaiah describe his mission?

What was the key to Isaiah's message?
Summarize Isaiah's prayer to God.

What was God's answer?

Discuss the sin progression demonstrated in these passages.

(2 Kings 19:37; 2 Chronicles 32:10, 33:10-17; Isaiah 37:38)
What happened to King Sennacherib of Assyria?

Who succeeded him as king?
What happened to King Manasseh of Judah?

How did King Manasseh respond?

How did God respond?

What did Manasseh do when he returned?

NAHUM'S PROPHECIES AND KING JOSIAH
(650–639 BC)
The Book of Nahum; 2 Kings 21:17–22:2, 23:26–27
2 Chronicles 33:18–34:2

Continue to complete your charts.

According to history, what happened to Sennacherib's army while laying siege to Jerusalem in 699 BC?

In 681 BC, what happened to Sennacherib?

Who became king of Assyria in 669 BC?

Describe the character of this king.

According to the book of Jonah, what was the attitude of the Ninevites 125 years ago?

Who was the king of Judah during the days of Nahum?
Why was God so angry at Nineveh?

What did Nahum prophesy about Nineveh?

When Manasseh died, who succeeded him as king of Judah?
How old was he?
How long did he reign in Jerusalem?
Describe the character of this king of Judah.

What happened to this king?
Who became the next king of Judah?
How old was he?
How long did he reign?
Describe the character of this king.

Describe God's relationship with Judah at this time.

ZEPHANIAH'S PROPHECIES
(635–625 BC)
The Book of Zephaniah

> *Continue to complete your charts.*

Who was God's prophet during this time?
Who was this prophet's great-great grandfather?
What judgment was prophesied against Judah?

What other nations were also to be punished?

What hope was prophesied for Judah?

JOSIAH'S REFORMS
(627 BC)
2 Chronicles 34:3–7

How old was King Josiah when he began to make sweeping religious reforms in Judah?

List some of the changes King Josiah made.

JEREMIAH'S PROPHECIES
(626–576 BC)
Jeremiah 1:1–20:13
2 Kings 22:3–23:28
2 Chronicles 34:8–35:19, 26–27

> *As you read through this section, look for warnings of impending doom for an unfaithful nation and evidence in support of the phrase, "Don't shoot the messenger!"*

Who was called to be God's prophet at this time?

Describe the time frame of his service.

When did God say He chose Jeremiah for His service?

Think about the purpose for which God has chosen you even before you were born.

What nickname has been given to this prophet?
When Jeremiah was afraid he wouldn't know what to say, how did God reassure him?

When Jeremiah wasn't sure what his message was to be, what did God show him?

How did Jeremiah compare God's people to a loving bride?

What charges did Jeremiah make against God's people?

How did God's people respond when warned by prophets like Jeremiah and given corrective punishment?

How did Jeremiah describe the behavior of God's people?

Who did Jeremiah use as an example for what would happen to a faithless and adulterous nation?

What invitation did God extend to Israel through Jeremiah?

Describe the conditions that were set.

What circumcision did God call Judah to perform?

What fall/disaster did Jeremiah prophesy for Judah?

What question did Jeremiah pose to God?

How did God respond?

What did God want from His people?

Discuss the implication for what God wants from us today.

What did Jeremiah prophesy about the temple?

How did God feel when forced to punish His people?

What reasons did Jeremiah give for why destruction had to take place?

How did Jeremiah say idols compared to God?

What covenant had been broken by the people of Judah?

How had the covenant been broken?
How did the men from Jeremiah's hometown react to his "hard preaching"?

What was to happen to these men as a result of their intentions?

Why was Jeremiah angry with God?

How did God respond?
What sign did God give Jeremiah?

What warnings did Jeremiah give?

Why did the people seek prophecy from other prophets?

Has there ever been a time when you struggled with listening to God's "hard truths"?

When Jeremiah prayed for a little mercy for the few faithful, how did God respond?

What constraints did God place on Jeremiah?

Why did Jeremiah tell the people they should observe the Sabbath Day?

How did God use a potter to deliver a message to Jeremiah?

What were the potter's plans?
What conspiracy was plotted against Jeremiah?

How did God use a clay jar as an object lesson for Judah?

What happened to Jeremiah when he returned after delivering this lesson?

What was to be the punishment for this action?

How did Jeremiah react when treated in this manner?

What did King Josiah do to the Lord's temple?

What was found in the temple?
What was done with this artifact?
What was the result of this action?

What major changes did King Josiah make?

What religious events were celebrated once again?

FALL OF ASSYRIA AND RISE OF BABYLON
(609–608 BC)
2 Kings 23:29–37; 2 Chronicles 35:20–36:5
Jeremiah 22:10–17, 26:1–23, 46:1–47:7

> *Continue to complete your charts.*

(Go to https://theologue.wordpress.com/2014/04/30/zaine-ridling-bible-atlas-e-book/. Use map 76, "The Rise of the Neo-Babylonian Empire," to track events that occurred during this time.)

Who rebelled against Assyria in 626 BC and established the Babylonian Empire?
What happened to the Assyrian city of Nineveh in 612 BC?

Who took his forces to Carchemish to try to stop this push for world dominance?

How did King Josiah respond to this army passing through his land?

What happened to King Josiah?

Who succeeded him as king of Judah?

How old was he?

How long did he reign in Jerusalem?

Describe the character of this king.

What happened to this king?

Who succeeded him as king of Judah?

How old was this new king of Judah?

How long was he the acting king?

Describe the character of this king.

What happened to Jeremiah when he once again prophesied about the destruction of Jerusalem?

Give Jeremiah's defense.

What was the outcome?

What happened to the prophet Uriah?

What prediction did Jeremiah make about Egypt in the battle at Carchemish?

What did happen to Egypt?

What promise did God make to Judah?

What did Jeremiah prophesy about the Philistines?

HABAKKUK
The Book of Habakkuk

> *As you read this prophecy, notice the unique questioning style used by this prophet and take note of God's answers.*

Who was Habakkuk?
What tough questions did Habakkuk ask?

How did the Lord answer Habakkuk?

How did Habakkuk respond to God's answer?

THE FIRST JUDEANS EXILED
(605–603 BC)
2 Kings 24:1, 7; 2 Chronicles 36:6–7
Jeremiah 25:1–38, 35:1–36:32, 45:1–5

> *Prophecy fulfilled!*

What epic battle took place at Carchemish in Mesopotamia?

During Jehoiakim's reign, who invaded Judah?
How long was Jehoiakim a puppet king?
Why didn't Egypt help Judah?

(Go to https://theologue.wordpress.com/2014/04/30/zaine-ridling-bible-atlas-e-book/. Use Map 78, "Nebuchadnezzar's Campaigns Against Judah," to track the battles that took place during this time.)

For the last twenty-three years, what has Jeremiah's prophecy been?

Who did the Lord use to bring His people to ruin?
What was to be Judah's punishment?

What was to happen to Judah's oppressor?

What nations had incurred the wrath of God?

What example did the Recabites demonstrate?

What command did God give concerning His message delivered through Jeremiah?

What two purposes did this command serve?

Who was the scribe for this project?
What was to be his compensation for this tedious effort?

Who read the scroll in the temple?
Why was a day of fasting chosen as the appropriate time for this reading?

Why didn't Jeremiah read the scroll in the temple?

What happened after the scroll was read to the officials?

What happened when the scroll was read to King Jehoiakim?

How did God respond to the king's actions?

DANIEL AND KING NEBUCHADNEZZAR
(604–597 BC)
Daniel 1:1–2:49; 2 Kings 24:1–6
Jeremiah 48:1–49:33, 22:18–23
2 Chronicles 36:8

> *As you read this section, look for acts of extreme faith. Also take note of how these hard choices were blessed by God. Continue to complete your charts.*

Where were some of the people of Judah at this time?

What qualities were required for service to this nation's king?

How were these men to be treated?
How long was their training period?
List four such men from Judah who were chosen to serve.

Identify the new Babylonian names given to each.

Why did Daniel refuse to eat the king's food?

Why were those supervising Daniel concerned about his refusal to eat the king's food?

What test was proposed?

What was the result of this test?

What special abilities did God give to these four?

Who did the king ask to interpret his dream?

What condition did the king place on his interpreters?

What would happen if these wise men could not comply?
How did these wise men respond?

What threat did the king issue?
Who offered to interpret the king's dream?
How was Daniel able to accomplish this feat?

Describe the king's dream.

Give the interpretation.

How did the king respond to this interpretation?

Against what nation did Jehoiakim rebel?
How did the Lord respond?

What was Jeremiah's prophecy concerning Judah's enemies?

What was Jeremiah's prophecy about Jehoiakim's death?

THE GREAT EXILE
(597 BC)
2 Kings 24:6–16; 2 Chronicles 36:8–10; Jeremiah 22:24–30; Daniel 1:1–2

(Go to https://theologue.wordpress.com/2014/04/30/zaine-ridling-bible-atlas-e-book/. Use Map 80, "Jewish Exiles in Babylonia," to track the route God's people took from Jerusalem to Babylon.)

Who succeeded Jehoiakim as king of Judah?
How old was he?
How long did he reign in Jerusalem?
Describe the character of this king.

Which of Jeremiah's prophecies did this king fulfill?

What finally happened to the people of Jerusalem in 597 BC?

What else was taken?

ZEDEKIAH AS KING
(597 BC)
2 Kings 24:17–20; 2 Chronicles 36:10–16
Jeremiah 37:1–2, 52:1–3

Continue to complete your charts.

Who succeeded Jehoiachin as the puppet king of Judah?

Identify the new Babylonian name given to him.
How old was he?
How long did he reign in Jerusalem?
Describe the character of this puppet king.

MORE PROPHECIES FROM JEREMIAH
(593 BC)
Jeremiah 24:1–10, 29:1–32, 27:1–28:17, 23:9–40, 50:1–51:64, 49:34–39, 34:8–22

What vision did God give Jeremiah?

Identify the main points of Jeremiah's letter to the exiles.

What did God ask Jeremiah to wear?
What message was being sent by this action?

What nations were targeted with this message?
Early on during the exile, who contradicted Jeremiah's message?
What was his prophecy?

How did Jeremiah respond?

What did Hananiah do to make his point?

How did God respond?

What was Jeremiah's prophecy about false prophets?

What message did God send to the exiles about what was to happen to Babylon?

What order did King Zedekiah give to the people left in Jerusalem?
How did the people respond to this order?

How did God respond?

EZEKIEL PROPHESIES FROM EXILE

(592–586 BC)

Ezekiel 1:1–23:49

> As you read through this section, look for comparisons between Jeremiah's prophecies to the people of Judah and Ezekiel's prophecies to the people in exile in Babylon. Continue to complete your charts.

Who was Ezekiel?

How old was Ezekiel when God called him to be His prophet?

How did God appear to Ezekiel?
Briefly describe (or make a sketch of) Ezekiel's vision.

Describe Ezekiel's reaction to this vision.

What did God tell Ezekiel to do?

Where was Ezekiel told to go?

What did God give Ezekiel to eat?
How did this object taste?
What difficulty was Ezekiel going to face?

Where did Ezekiel go next?
How long was Ezekiel in a state of feeling totally overwhelmed?
What was the Lord's message to Ezekiel after this time was up?

Describe and explain the first sign God gave to Ezekiel.

Describe and explain the second sign.

(Use building bricks or clay to re-create this sign.)

Describe and explain the third sign.

Describe and explain the fourth sign.

Describe and explain the fifth sign.

After God destroyed Israel because of her idolatry, who was left?

What day had finally arrived?

Where was Ezekiel at this time?
How did Ezekiel get to Jerusalem?

What did Ezekiel see in the temple?

Why did God call on the guards of the city?

Who was spared?

What did Ezekiel see next?

How did Ezekiel get to the east door of the temple?
What happened while Ezekiel was prophesying against the city's corrupt leaders?

Why was Ezekiel so upset?
What promise did God make to Ezekiel?

How did Ezekiel get back to Babylonia?

What two messages from God did Ezekiel act out for those already exiled in Babylonia?

Why didn't the people show more concern about what was being prophesied by God's messengers like Ezekiel?

How did God handle this problem?

Who were the main contributors to this problem?

Name the three men who, even in all their righteousness, would not have been able to stop Judah's upcoming judgment.
How did Ezekiel describe Judah's certain destruction?

How did Ezekiel describe what was going to happen to King Zedekiah?

What did the Lord say He would do with the top of His cedar tree?

Explain what Ezekiel meant by "The one who sins is the one who will die." (Ezekiel 18:20)

What would happen if a wicked man repented?

What would happen if a righteous man became wicked?

Ezekiel wrote a lament for two of Judah's kings. Who were they?

When the elders of Israel came to see him, what did Ezekiel have to tell?

What message of hope did Ezekiel have for them?

What message of judgment did Ezekiel have for Judah?

What message of judgment did Ezekiel have for Jerusalem and the land of Israel?

What message of judgment did Ezekiel have for King Zedekiah?

Make a list of Jerusalem's sins.

> *Discussion: Which of these sins still exist today?*

What was to be Jerusalem's punishment?

What kind of person was God looking for?

> *Discussion: Are you this kind of person?*

Who did God find?
Describe Ezekiel's comparison of God's people to two promiscuous sisters.

THE SIEGE OF JERUSALEM
(590–588 BC)
2 Kings 24:20–25:1; 2 Chronicles 36:13
Jeremiah 52:3–4; 39:1; Ezekiel 24:1–27

Meanwhile, back in Jerusalem, what did the puppet king Zedekiah decide to do?

What was the result of his decision?

When did this event occur?

In Tel Abib, Babylonia, what date did God tell Ezekiel to record? Why?

Why did Ezekiel's wife die?

Describe the conditions God put on Ezekiel. Why?

PROPHECIES FROM JEREMIAH ABOUT A SPIRITUAL RESTORATION
(587 BC)
Jeremiah 21:1–22:9, 34:1–7, 32:1–33:13, 30:1–31:26
23:1–8, 33:14–26, 31:27–40

Look for all the "good news" messages as you read through this section.

Describe what happened when an opposing army laid siege to a city.

During the siege of Jerusalem, what advice did Jeremiah give to Zedekiah?

Why were Judah's evil kings being punished?

What choice did Zedekiah make?
What was Jeremiah's prophecy about Zedekiah?

What was Zedekiah's response to this prophecy?
What message was in Jeremiah's story about purchasing a field?

What was God's charge against Jerusalem?

What promise did God make?

What was Jeremiah's prophecy about the houses and royal palaces of Jerusalem?

What promises did God make?

What did God tell Jeremiah to do to ensure God would be given proper credit when these promises came true?

What words of encouragement did Jeremiah have for the captives in Ramah?

What did God promise to do with the remnant of His flock?

What leadership did God promise to provide?

Describe the new covenant that was to be established.

EZEKIEL'S SIEGE PROPHECIES FROM BABYLON
(588–586 BC)
Ezekiel 25:1–17, 29:1–16, 30:1–31:18, 26:1–28:26

What nations were singled out for judgment because they oppressed God's people and then gloated and celebrated over their downfall?
What individual drew God's wrath?
What cities also drew God's wrath?
Who was God going to use to bring these cities down?
Why was God so angry at the king of one of these cities?

Why was God so angry at these two cities?

What was to be accomplished by these judgments?

Sixteen years later, who had laid a thirteen-year siege to one of these cities?

JEREMIAH'S DEATH THREAT IN JERUSALEM
Jeremiah 37:3–38:28

Why did the Babylonian army withdraw from their siege of Jerusalem?

When this occurred, what did the people of Jerusalem think?
What was Jeremiah's prophecy about this situation?

Why was Jeremiah arrested, beaten, and put in prison?

Who rescued Jeremiah from his dungeon cell?

Why were the city officials so upset with Jeremiah?

What did they want to do with Jeremiah?

What did they do to Jeremiah?

Who pleaded to King Zedekiah for Jeremiah's release?

Once freed, who sent for Jeremiah? Why?
Why was Jeremiah so hesitant about responding to this request?

What was Jeremiah's answer to the king's question?

What did King Zedekiah ask of Jeremiah?

Where did Jeremiah go next?

JERUSALEM FALLS
(586–582 BC)
2 Kings 25:2–22; 2 Chronicles 36:17–21
Jeremiah 38: 2-8, 52: 5-30, 39: 2-18, 40 :1-6

In the eleventh year of King Zedekiah's reign, what happened to the city of Jerusalem?

How did King Zedekiah react?

What happened to King Zedekiah?

What happened to Jerusalem one month later?

How long were the Judeans exiled in Babylon?
Who did Nebuchadnezzar appoint as governor of Judah?
What was Jeremiah's fate? Why?

LAMENTATIONS
(586 BC)
The Book of Lamentations

As you read this poem, think about all the choices God's people made. Even after countless warnings, the end result was as prophesied, yet there was hope.

Who wrote Lamentations?
What are "lamentations"?
Make a list of the lamentations expressed in this poem.

What still gave the writer hope?

A REMNANT ESCAPES TO EGYPT

(586 BC)

2 Kings 25:23–26; Jeremiah 40:7–44:30, 51:64

(Go to https://theologue.wordpress.com/2014/04/30/zaine-ridling-bible-atlas-e-book/. Use Map 81, "Jewish Refugees in Egypt," to track the flight of the remnant that escaped from Jerusalem.)

Who came to meet with Gedaliah at Mizpah?

What did these men want?
What did Gedaliah tell them?

Who returned to Judah?
What warning did Johanan son of Kareah give to Gedaliah?

How did Gedaliah react?

What happened to Gedaliah?

What happened the next day?

Who went to rescue the people of Mizpah?

Where did they catch up with Ishmael?
What happened at this place?

Why was this remnant afraid to return to Judah?

Where did they go instead?
Along the way, who did they ask for direction?
What promise did this group make?
What did God want this remnant to do?
What would happen if they decided not to do as God wanted?

How did they respond to Jeremiah's message from God?

What did they decide to do?

What prophecy did God give to Jeremiah in Tahpanhes, Egypt?

What warning did God have for the Jews in Egypt?

How did the Jewish men respond?

What did Jeremiah say was Judah's downfall?

What judgment was coming?

What did Jeremiah prophesy would happen to the current pharaoh of Egypt?

The Israelite Nation in Exile

(585–535 BC)

> As you read this section, look for prophecy about God's new covenant of peace with His people. Be able to identify the ways in which this new covenant is different from the old one.

EZEKIEL PROPHESIES ABOUT A RESTORATION
(586 BC)
Ezekiel 33:21–39:29, 32:1–33:20

What happened in the twelfth year of the Babylonian exile?

What happened to Ezekiel the night before this visit?

What happened the morning of the visit? Why?

Why did God say the people lost possession of Canaan?

Explain Ezekiel's comparison of God's people to a flock of sheep.

Why was Edom to be punished?

What was Ezekiel's prophecy about Israel's future?

How did Ezekiel say God's people would be new?

What was the message of Ezekiel's vision of a valley full of dry bones?

Explain the message of the sign of the two sticks.

Who was to be the "one king" of this new kingdom?

Describe Ezekiel's prophecy against Gog of the land of Magog.

For what nation did Ezekiel lament? Why?

Explain how Ezekiel's prophet role was like the job of a watchman.

How did Ezekiel say God felt about punishing people?

SHADRACH, MESHACH, AND ABEDNEGO
(584 BC?)
Daniel 3:1–30

What new command did King Nebuchadnezzar put into effect?

What action did some astrologers take?

How did the king respond?

How did Shadrach, Meshach, and Abednego respond?

Discuss a time when you faced a situation where you were asked to deny God. What was your attitude? What was your mind-set?

How did the king react to the decision of these three men?

What did King Nebuchadnezzar see when he looked into the fiery furnace?

What was the king's response?

Describe Shadrach, Meshach, and Abednego's condition.

What was the result of this miraculous event?

EZEKIEL'S TEMPLE VISION AND HIS DEATH
(572–570 BC)
Ezekiel 40:1–48:35, 29:17–21

> *Try to picture Ezekiel's temple as you read through this section. Continue to complete your charts.*

When was Ezekiel taken back to Israel?

How did he travel?
Who did Ezekiel see from his position on a very high mountain?

What did this man do?

In general terms, how big was this structure?

When Ezekiel reached the east gate, what entered this structure?

What was promised?

Why was Ezekiel supposed to share his vision with the people of Israel?

Why was the east gate to remain shut?

Who was still not allowed to enter this structure? Why?

What limitations were placed on the Levites? Why?

Which priests were still in favor with God? Why?

What clothing restrictions were placed on the priests?

What other restrictions were placed on priests?

What civic duty were the priests to perform?

Who would perform the typical high priest's temple duties?
What feasts would still be celebrated?
What special days would still be celebrated?
After describing all the different offerings, what did the man show Ezekiel?

How was the land to be divided?

What was the name of the city?
What did God say King Nebuchadnezzar's reward would be for his unsuccessful thirteen-year siege against Tyre?

NEBUCHADNEZZAR'S INSANITY
(562–561 BC?)
Daniel 4:1–37

Describe King Nebuchadnezzar's dream.

Describe Daniel's interpretation.

A year later, what triggered this dream to become reality?

What happened to the king?

What caused this nightmare to end?

How long did King Nebuchadnezzar rule Babylon?
(2 Kings 25: 27-30; Jeremiah 52: 31-34)
Who succeeded him as king?
What happened in the thirty-seventh year of the exile?

Where was the last known residence of Jeremiah?

THE STORY OF JOB
The Book of Job

As you read this story, consider the timeless message it delivers about adversity, pain, and suffering and God's role through it all.

Who was Job?

Give an example of Job's righteousness.

What reason did Satan give for Job's faithfulness to God?

What challenge did Satan issue to God regarding Job?

How did God respond?

What reports did the four messengers have for Job?

How did Job respond?

> *Discussion: Have you ever been in a similar situation? What was your response? Why is Job's response so difficult to emulate?*

What second challenge did Satan issue?

How did God respond?

What happened to Job?

Who encouraged Job to stop believing in God?
How did Job respond to this person?

Who came to sympathize with Job and to try to comfort him?

After seven days and seven nights of suffering, what did Job do?

What advice did Eliphaz give?

How did Job describe his present physical state?

What was Bildad's advice?

What was Job's reply?

What insight did Zophar give?

How did Job respond?

Why did Eliphaz rebuke Job?

How did Job feel about his friends' "help"?

> *Discussion: Have your friends ever made you feel this way? Have you ever had this effect on one of your friends?*

How did Bildad respond to Job's indictment?

What was Job's reply?

What did Zophar have to say after hearing Job's defense?

How did Job respond?

How did Eliphaz answer Job?

How did Job respond?

In what way did Bildad agree with Eliphaz?

How did Job describe the effect of his friends' words?

Why did Job reaffirm his faith?

How did Job describe God's wisdom?

How did Job describe his previous status?

How did Job describe his present situation?

Who weighed in with his opinion of Job?
Why was this person so angry?

What advice did he give Job?

After all this discussion, what questions did God ask?

What was Job's reaction?
What additional question did God have for Job?

Now what did Job have to say?

What did God have to say to Job's friends?

Describe Job's final condition.

EXILE PSALMS
Psalm 44, 74, 79, 80, 85, 89, 102, 106, 123, 137

Make a list of the central themes found in this group of ten psalms.

DANIEL'S VISIONS
(552–542 BC)
Daniel 7:1–8:27, 5:1–31, 9:1–27

> *Be able to identify the themes found in Daniel's visions. Continue to complete your prophet chart.*

Who was the king of Babylon at this time?

Describe Daniel's dream of the four beasts.

Explain the interpretation of this beast dream.

Describe Daniel's vision of the ram and the goat.

Explain the interpretation of this ram/goat vision.

How did these visions affect Daniel?

During one of his great banquets, how did Belshazzar dishonor God?

What mystical event occurred?

What was Belshazzar's reaction?

Who was called to come and interpret this event?

What was offered if successful?
Who did the queen say could help?
What reward did Daniel want?

Explain Daniel's interpretation of the writing on the wall.

What did Belshazzar do for Daniel?

What happened to Belshazzar that very night?

How long had the exiles been in Babylonian captivity?
How did Daniel know the exile would last seventy years?

Describe Daniel's prayer.

What happened while Daniel was praying?

What was this angel's message?

DANIEL IN THE LIONS' DEN
(541–540 BC)
Daniel 6:1–28

What rank did Daniel hold in Darius the Mede's kingdom?

What promotion was Daniel to receive? Why?

How did the other government officials feel about Daniel's promotion?

Why were they unsuccessful?

What did they identify as Daniel's only weakness?
What plot did they devise?

What did Daniel do?

> *Discussion: How do you think you would respond to a "lions' den" challenge to your faith?*

Who ran to tell the king?
How did the king respond to the news?

What happened the next morning?

What was Daniel's response?

What happened to Daniel's accusers?

What decree did King Darius issue?

Who became the next king of Babylonia?

Restoration: Another New Beginning

(535–425 BC)

> As you read through this section, look for evidence of how God never gives up on His relationship with His people.

THE RETURN TO JERUSALEM

(539–538 BC)

Ezra 1:1–4:5; 2 Chronicles 36:22–23

(Go to https://theologue.wordpress.com/2014/04/30/zaine-ridling-bible-atlas-e-book/. Use Map 85, "The Return of Jewish Exiles to Judah," to track the route God's people took as they came back to Jerusalem.)

Who was the new ruler over the exiled nation of Israel?
During his first year as king, what proclamation did he issue?

What motivated some Jews to return to Judah?
What assistance was given?

How did the king help?

Who was the leader of the first great migration back to Judah?
How many exiles were in this group?
After they settled in their own towns, what did this group do?

When was the temple foundation laid?

Why were some upset during this momentous occasion?

How did outsiders "help"?

DANIEL'S FINAL VISION
(536 BC)
Daniel 10:1–12:13

As Daniel stood on the banks of the Tigris River, who did he see?

Describe Daniel's reaction to this vision.

Why had this man come to Daniel?

Describe the events foretold by this vision.

When would these last events be fulfilled?
What was to happen to Daniel?

PROBLEMS WITH TEMPLE CONSTRUCTION
(529–520 BC)
Ezra 4:6–6:13

Who was the current king of Persia?

What accusation was lodged against the Jews?

How did the king respond?
What happened back in Jerusalem?
Once Darius became king, who restarted the temple work?

When did this occur?
Who was the current governor?
How did King Darius respond to a letter questioning his authority to rebuild the temple?

PROPHECIES OF HAGGAI AND ZECHARIAH

(520–518 BC)

The Book of Haggai; Zechariah 1:1–8:23

> *Look for encouraging messages from these two prophets and continue to complete your prophet chart.*

Who was the current governor?

Who was the high priest?

Who was the Lord's prophet?

What message did this prophet have for God's people?

What effect did his words have on the people?

What message did this prophet have for those who remembered the glory of the old temple?

> *Discussion: Who do you think is the greater glory and peace that will one day fill the new temple?*

Who else prophesied at this time?

What warning did this prophet give?

What was the significance of being God's "signet ring"?

ZECHARIAH'S EIGHT VISIONS

	VISION	GOD'S MESSAGE
First		
Second		
Third		
Fourth		
Fifth		
Sixth		
Seventh		
Eighth		

Fill in the chart of Zechariah's eight visions.

Describe Zechariah's first vision.

What was the message to God's people?

Describe Zechariah's second vision.
What was the message to God's people?

Describe Zechariah's third vision.
What was the message to God's people?

Describe Zechariah's fourth vision.

What was the message to God's people?

Discussion: Who is the "Branch" who will remove all sin?

Describe Zechariah's fifth vision.

What was God's message?

Describe Zechariah's sixth vision.
What was God's message?
Describe Zechariah's seventh vision.

What was God's message?

Describe Zechariah's eighth vision.

What was God's message?

Discuss how the messages of these eight visions apply to believers today.

What directive did God give to Zechariah?

What question did the people of Bethel have?

How did God answer through Zechariah?

How did Zechariah motivate those who were rebuilding the temple?

What did God ask in return?

Discussion: Does God desire anything different from our worship today? Why or why not?

What would be the outcome of lives lived for God in this way?

Discussion: Is this outcome any different today? Why or why not?

What effect did the preaching of Haggai and Zechariah have on the temple work?

TEMPLE CONSTRUCTION COMPLETED
(516 BC)
Ezra 6:14–22

In what year was the temple construction completed?
How many years had it been since Solomon's temple was destroyed?
Describe the dedication ceremony of the rebuilt temple.

PSALMS OF A RESTORED NATION
Psalm 78, 107, 116, 118, 125, 126, 128, 129, 132, 147, 149

List the themes found in this group of eleven psalms.

Discuss how these psalms also express the present day feelings of God's people.

MORE PROPHECIES FROM ZECHARIAH
(460 BC?)
Zechariah 9:1–14:21

As you read through these prophecies, look for specific and detailed predictions about the coming Messiah.

What did Zechariah prophesy would happen to Israel's oppressors?

How did Zechariah describe the coming of the king of Zion?

What was the prophesied price of broken favor with God?

What was the result of broken union with God?

Who will be mourned and bitterly grieved?

What will be opened "on that day"?

What will happen to the people "on that day"?

THE STORY OF ESTHER
(483-479 B.C.?)
The Book of Esther

Look for ironies throughout this story.

Who was the current king of Persia?

Where did this story take place?

What event was the king hosting?

Who was the queen?

Why did the king command the queen to appear?

How did the queen respond?

What effect did her decision have on the king?

What were the consequences of the queen's decision?

Who was Mordecai?

Who was his cousin?
Why was Mordecai taking care of this woman?

Why was Esther taken to the citadel at Susa?

Why did Esther keep her nationality and background a secret?

What was the king's first reaction to Esther?

What favor did Mordecai perform for King Xerxes?

Who was Haman?

Describe Mordecai's relationship with Haman.

How did Haman respond to Mordecai's treatment of him?

What plot did Haman devise?

How did Mordecai react to the news of this new decree?

Why was Esther hesitant to comply with Mordecai's request?

What did Mordecai say to encourage Esther?

Discussion: Have you ever felt you were placed in a certain position for a specific reason?

What did Esther decide to do?

How did Esther gain access to the king?

What was Esther's request?
Describe Haman's mood following the first event.

What suggestion did Haman's wife and friends make?

That night, what happened to King Xerxes?

When asked for his opinion, what presumption did Haman make?

Based on this presumption, what answer did Haman give?

How did King Xerxes respond to Haman's suggestion?

What happened at the second banquet hosted by Queen Esther?

Describe the king's reaction

What new order did the king issue?

Describe Mordecai's new status.

How did the Jews receive this new decree?

What day of celebration was established to commemorate these historical events?

MALACHI'S PROPHECIES

(500–460 BC?)

The Book of Malachi

As you read through this section, fill in the chart of Malachi's prophecies with statements of affirmation/given truths, doubters' questions, foolishness of questions, and God's answers.

MALACHI'S PROPHECIES

Given Truth	Questions	Foolishness	Answers

What happened to King Xerxes?
Who succeeded him as king?
Describe the mood of the Jews back in Israel.

How was Malachi's style of prophecy different from all the other prophets?

EZRA AND THE SECOND GROUP OF EXILES
(458 BC)
Ezra 7:1–10:44

Who led the second group of exiles back to Palestine?
Describe this man.

How did King Artaxerxes support this trip?

Why were no soldiers provided to protect a group carrying so much gold and silver?

What did the travelers do before they departed?

How long did the journey take?
How were they able to travel so quickly?

How many Jews were in this second travel party?
Why was intermarriage such an important issue?

Describe the Jews' reaction when they heard Ezra's prayer.

How did Ezra judiciously handle this matter?

How long did this process take?
Describe the outcome of Ezra's solution.

NEHEMIAH

The Rebuilding of the Wall around Jerusalem
(445–444 BC)
Nehemiah 1:1–6:16

What news came from Jerusalem?

Who received this news?
How did this man respond?

What position did this man hold?

Who noticed Nehemiah's sadness?
Why was Nehemiah so sad?
What requests did Nehemiah make of the king?

How did the king respond?

Who was not happy to see Nehemiah?
Why were these two so disturbed?

What did Nehemiah do during the night?

Once the wall-rebuilding plan was revealed, who led the mocking and ridicule?

Describe how the rebuilding plan was instituted.

What effect did the taunts and threats begin to have?

Describe Nehemiah's plan to thwart this psychological attack.

What new problem arose?

What promise did the noblemen make?

Describe the example set by Nehemiah.

How many times did the schemers ask to meet with Nehemiah?
What happened the last time when they asked for a meeting?

Describe the ploy devised in an attempt to discredit Nehemiah.

What else did Tobiah do to undermine Nehemiah's efforts?

How long did it take to rebuild the wall?
Describe the effect the wall's completion had on the Jews' enemies.

The Redistribution of the Population
(444 BC)
Nehemiah 7:1–12:26

Who did Governor Nehemiah put in charge of Jerusalem?
Who was appointed commander of the citadel?

What problem did Nehemiah face?

How did Nehemiah solve this problem?

Who was the high priest at this time?

After all the people were settled in their towns, why were all the men and women assembled in the square in Jerusalem?

Who helped with instruction?
How did the people respond?

What did Governor Nehemiah say to encourage them?

What feast was celebrated?

Describe what happened twenty-two days later.

In their confessional prayer, how did the Levites describe God?

What did the Jews do after confessing their sins?

Which commands did the Jews specifically promise to obey?

The Reform of Religious Practices
(425 BC?)
Nehemiah 13:4–31, 12:27–13:3

Who was the high priest at this time?
How did this high priest desecrate the temple?

Where was Nehemiah?

What issues did Nehemiah deal with upon his return to Jerusalem?

Describe the wall dedication celebration.

How did this celebration end?

ISRAEL'S OFFICIAL RECORDS
1 Chronicles 1:1–9:34

> *As you read through these official records, see if you*
> *can trace the genealogy of Jesus Christ.*

Why were genealogical records so important?

Where did this official record begin?

Which two well-known nations descended from Ham?

Which famous patriarch descended from Shem?

What nation descended from Esau?

What nation descended from Jacob?

Name the two most famous kings who descended from Judah?

From what clan was Samuel?

When did the official record of high priests begin?

From what clan was Joshua, the son of Nun?

Why do you think the genealogies of priests and kings were included?

The Time between the Testaments

(425–5 BC)

> *Review God's first covenant with Abraham and recall how this promise was broken by the Israelites. Be able to define what is meant by "apocryphal" writings. Be able to identify and describe the books that make up the Apocrypha. Be able to briefly describe Greek and Roman influences on the Jewish nation.*

AT THE END OF THE OLD TESTAMENT

What three-part promise did God give to Abraham?

What was God's first covenant with His people?

What was the first written symbol of this covenant?
What caused the Israelites to wander in the desert for forty years?

How were they finally able to enter the Promised Land?

In the beginning, how were the Israelites governed?
How long were they ruled by kings?
What happened to the kingdom after Solomon died?

Summarize what happened to the Israelites over the next 325 years.

Who did God send to try to warn His people?
How long did the exile last?
How long did it take the Jews to rebuild the temple in Jerusalem?
What nation ruled the Jews in 425 BC?
What great questions remained unanswered?

How long did the historical record of Scripture lie silent?
How many writings are in the Old Testament?
How many writings make up the New Testament?

THE APOCRYPHAL WRITINGS

What does the word *apocrypha* mean?
When were these historical and/or religious documents written?

What is the Greek version of the Old Testament called?

In what text did the Apocrypha first appear?
In what texts do these writings appear today?

Why are the writings of the Apocrypha not included in all Bibles?

List the writings that make up the Apocrypha. Briefly describe each.

THE JEWS AND THE GREEKS

(Information from this section is taken from *The Narrated Bible in Chronological Order*, narrated by F. LaGard Smith, NIV version (Eugene: Harvest House, 1984), 1343–1348.)

Make a list of some of the influences on those Jews who chose not to return to Judea.

What religious building replaced the temple?
Who replaced the priest?
Describe what is meant by "remnant theology."

When did the Persian Empire finally fall?
Who conquered the Persian Empire?
Who destroyed the city of Tyre?

What new city took its place on the Nile?
What culture had a profound effect on the Jews in Egypt and Palestine?

When did Alexander the Great die?
Who took over after his death?

Who captured Jerusalem?
Where did he send a number of Jews?

What text did Ptolemy II commission?
In 190 BC, what emerging world power defeated the Seleucid king of Palestine, Antiochus III?
What was the result of the pact with Antiochus IV?

Who was the next Seleucid ruler of Palestine?
How did he treat the Jews?

Who rose up against this terrible king?

In 135 BC, who finally became the ruler of Palestine?

THE JEWS AND THE ROMANS
(Information from this section is taken from *The Narrated Bible in Chronological Order,* narrated by F. LaGard Smith, NIV version (Eugene: Harvest House, 1984), 1343–1348.)

What happened in 63 BC?

Who defeated this general?
Who was appointed procurator over all Judea?
After his assassination, who was appointed tetrarch of Galilee?
Who revolted against this leader?
Who helped this ruler reestablish his position by naming him king of Judea and taking back control of the country?
What famous Ptolemaic (Egyptian) woman married this man?
What happened to this couple in 31 BC?

In 27 BC, what title did the Roman senate give to Octavian?
Who restored the temple in Jerusalem?
What Jewish religious sects gained prominence during this time? Briefly describe each.

A New Covenant through Christ: The Beginning of the Gospel Message

(5 BC–30 AD)

> As you read this section, look for evidence of God's amazing love and proof that He always keeps His promises. Also, be able to explain God's new covenant, which provides for the salvation of all people through God's Son, Jesus.

THE BIRTH OF JESUS AND JOHN THE BAPTIST

Matthew 1:1–25; Mark 1:1

Luke 1:1–2:38, 3:23–28

John 1:1–18

What momentous event was about to occur?

When was this event planned?

What was so unique about this event?

What four books of the Bible tell the story of Jesus?

Who did Mark say Jesus was?

How did John describe Jesus?

How did John describe himself?

How did Luke describe himself?

How did Matthew's account of the life of Jesus begin?

How many generations were there from Abraham to David, from David to the exile, and from the exile to Christ's birth?

How did Luke trace the genealogy of Jesus?

Make a list of the common ancestors found in these two genealogies.

Explain the significance of both genealogies tracing back through King David.

(Go to https://theologue.wordpress.com/2014/04/30/zaine-ridling-bible-atlas-e-book/. Use Map 102, "The Division of Herod's Kingdom," to identify the Roman kings who were in power during this time and to locate their kingdoms.)
(Go to www.wikipedia.org/wiki/Herod_the_Great#Family_trees/. Scroll down through the article and click on # 9, Family Trees, in the content box. Use this diagram to learn about the house of Herod.)

Palestine was divided into five provinces. Name them.

In which province were the cities of Jerusalem and Bethlehem?
In which province was the city of Nazareth?
Who was the king of Judea at this time?

Who was a priest during this time?
What was his wife's name?
What problem did he and his wife have?
What message did the angel of the Lord bring to this priest?

How was this future son described?

What was the angel of the Lord's name?
What price did the priest pay for his disbelief?
What happened during the sixth month of Elizabeth's pregnancy?

What was the angel's message this time?

Discuss Mary's role as the teenage mother of God in the flesh, the Savior of the world.

Who did Mary go to see?
Describe the reaction of Elizabeth's unborn child when he heard Mary's greeting.

How long did Mary stay?
What happened on the eighth day after Elizabeth gave birth?

What happened when Zechariah wrote down the name of his newborn son?

What did Zechariah prophesy about his newborn son's future?

Where did John live?
What was Joseph's reaction when he heard Mary was pregnant?

Discuss the role of Joseph as foster father to God's only Son.

Who appeared to Joseph in a dream?
What was the message?

What decree did Caesar Augustus issue?

Where did Joseph and Mary go? Why?

What monumental event occurred here?
Describe the setting for this miraculous event.

Discuss the significance of this site for such a momentous event.

Why was the child born here?
What happened to terrify the nearby shepherds?

What was the message?

What amazing thing suddenly happened?

What did the shepherds do?

What happened on the eighth day after Mary gave birth?

What did Joseph and Mary do with Jesus as an act of obedience to the Law of Moses?

How did Simeon react when the baby Jesus arrived?

Who else was at the temple that day?

What was this woman's reaction to the arrival of the baby Jesus?

JESUS'S FLIGHT TO EGYPT
Matthew 2:1–18

(Go to https://theologue.wordpress.com/2014/04/30/zaine-ridling-bible-atlas-e-book/. Use Map 105, "Jesus' Birth and Early Childhood," to trace His early travels.)

Who came from the east to Jerusalem seeking the "newborn king"?

How did these men know where to go to find this king?
How did King Herod react when he heard who these men wanted to find?

How did King Herod know where to look for Jesus?

How did King Herod try to use the magi?

When the magi found Jesus, what gifts did they present to Him?

Why didn't the magi report back to King Herod?

Who appeared to Joseph in a dream?
What was the message?

How did King Herod respond when he realized the magi had outwitted him?

THE EARLY YEARS OF JESUS
Matthew 2:19–23; Luke 2:39–52

How did Joseph know it was safe to return to Israel?

Who was the current king of Judea?
Where did the family go to live?

Why did the family travel to Jerusalem each year?
When Jesus was twelve years old, what happened on this trip?

How long was Jesus missing?

When He was found, what was Jesus doing?

Describe the reaction of His parents when they found Jesus.

How did Jesus respond?

What was the family trade?
List four of Jesus's brothers.

JOHN THE BAPTIST'S MINISTRY
(October, 27 AD)
Matthew 3:1–17; Mark 1:2–11; Luke 3:1–23

Who was the reigning Caesar at this time?
Who was the governor of Judea?
Who was the tetrarch of Galilee?

Why is mention made of the political leaders during this time in history?

Who were the high priests?
Who was preaching in the area around the Jordan River?

What was his message?
Describe this preacher.

What advice did he have for Jews, tax collectors, and soldiers?

What "good news" did this man preach?

Compare John's baptism with Jesus's baptism.

Who came to John to be baptized? Why?

What happened when Jesus came up out of the water?

How old was Jesus when He began His ministry?

SATAN'S TEMPTATION OF JESUS
Matthew 4:1–11; Mark 1:12–13
Luke 4:1–13; John 1: 19–34

In this section, look for evidence of the deity and humanity of Jesus.

Who led Jesus into the desert?
Why was He led there?
How long did Jesus fast?
Describe the first temptation of Jesus.

How did Jesus deal with this first temptation?

Describe the second temptation.

How did Jesus deal with this temptation?

Describe the third temptation.

How did Jesus respond this time?

When the devil left, who came to care for Jesus?
How did John describe himself?

Where was John when Jesus came to see him?
How did John describe Jesus?

JESUS'S EARLY MINISTRY
(27 AD)
John 1:35–4:54
Luke 3:19–20

> *As you read this section, take note of the miracles of Jesus as well as their intended purposes. Also look for evidence that proves "the gospel is for all."*

(Go to https://theologue.wordpress.com/2014/04/30/zaine-ridling-bible-atlas-e-book/. Use Map 107, "Galilee in the Time of Jesus," to follow Jesus during the early years of His ministry.)

Who were the first two disciples to follow Jesus?

Who was the next person to follow Jesus?
Name the hometown of these first three disciples.
Who was the next man to be told to come follow Jesus?

How did this man respond when he learned the name of Jesus's hometown?

Describe the first miracle performed by Jesus.

What was the result of this miracle?

Where was Jesus going in April of 27 AD? Why?

What did Jesus find in the temple courts?

What did Jesus do about this situation?

What miraculous sign did Jesus say He could perform to prove He had the authority to run the merchants out of "His Father's house"?

Why did this feat seem so impossible?

What "temple" was Jesus talking about?
Who came to see Jesus one night?

What teaching did Jesus give this man?

Why was His message so confusing?

What rebirth did Jesus mean?

Who did Jesus say had come from heaven?
What had to happen to Jesus before eternal life could be achieved?

Why did Jesus say God had devised this plan of salvation?

What were Jesus and John both doing in the Judean countryside?
What argument arose?

How did John handle this issue?

Where did Jesus and His disciples go next?
As He traveled through Sychar, Samaria, where did Jesus stop to rest?

Where were His disciples?
Who came to draw water?
What did Jesus ask of her?
Why was this request so unusual?

What teaching did Jesus give this woman?

How did the woman respond to His message?

What did Jesus tell her to do?
Why did this request present a problem for her?

What teaching did Jesus give this woman concerning the proper place to worship?

When she returned to town, what did the woman tell people?

What was the result of her testimony?

Describe the second miracle performed by Jesus in Cana, Galilee.

Why did Herod put John the Baptist in prison?

JESUS'S GREAT MINISTRY IN GALILEE
Matthew 4:12–25, 8:1–4, 14–17, 9:1–17, 12:1–21
Mark 1:14–3:19; Luke 4:14–6:19; John 5:1–3, 5–47

(Go to https://theologue.wordpress.com/2014/04/30/zaine-ridling-bible-atlas-e-book/. Use Map 108, "The Ministry of Jesus around the Sea of Galilee," to follow Jesus during this time of His ministry.)

Where was Jesus when He heard about John's imprisonment?
Where did Jesus go to live and set up His ministry?

On a return trip to Nazareth, what happened when Jesus went to the synagogue?

Describe the reaction of those in attendance.

How did Jesus escape?
What miracle did Jesus perform on Lake Gennesaret (Sea of Galilee)?

Name Simon Peter's fishing partners.

What new role did Jesus give these fishermen?

What miracle did Jesus perform at the synagogue in Capernaum?

Which relative of Peter's did Jesus heal?
What happened that evening?

What did Jesus do before the sun was up the next morning?
What warning did Jesus give after healing the man with leprosy?

What did the man do instead?
What was the result of this man's actions?

How did the paralytic's friends get him through the crowd that was packed in the home where Jesus was preaching?

How did Jesus respond?

Why did Jesus's statement about forgiving sins lead some Scribes to question Him?

Why was it so important for Jesus to make this statement?

Who was the next man to be called to follow Jesus?

What did this man do to honor Jesus?

What problem did the Pharisees and Scribes have with those in attendance?

How did Jesus respond?

Why did Jesus say His disciples did not fast like John's did?

Explain the parable of the new patch on the old wineskin.

Why did Jesus go up to Jerusalem?

Who typically gathered near the Sheep Gate by a pool called Bethesda?

Why did these people lie by this pool?

Who did Jesus heal here?
What did Jesus say to this man?

On what day did this healing occur?
Why did some of the Jews persecute Jesus?

What did they want to do to Jesus?
How did Jesus respond to their questions?

Why did the Pharisees criticize Jesus's disciples for plucking grain to eat?

How did Jesus respond to their accusation?

What other action did Jesus take on a Sabbath even though He knew the Pharisees were just looking for a reason to accuse Him?
How did the Pharisees respond?

Name the twelve disciples who were chosen by Jesus to be His apostles.

Why were such great crowds gathering around Jesus?

JESUS'S SERMON ON THE MOUNT
Matthew 5:1–7:29; Luke 6:20–49

As you read the greatest sermon ever delivered, think about how the teachings of Jesus can be applied to your life.

What blessings did Jesus say the "poor in spirit" would receive?

What will happen to those who feel godly sorrow?
What blessings are in store for the meek?

How will God treat those who hunger and thirst for righteousness?

How will the merciful be treated?
What is in store for those who have a pure heart?
What will the peacemakers be called?
What will happen to those who are persecuted because they seek righteousness?

How should a believer respond when he is insulted, persecuted, and lied about because he follows Jesus?

What warnings are given about impending sorrow?

How did Jesus describe the nature of His believers?

How did Jesus's teaching improve on the sixth commandment?

How did Jesus's teaching improve on the seventh commandment?

Under what condition did Jesus say divorce could be attained without causing sin?
What was Jesus's teaching about swearing an oath to back up a verbal commitment?

What was Jesus's teaching about retaliation?

What was Jesus's teaching about love?

Discussion: Why is this type of love so difficult?

How did Jesus say acts of charity should be conducted?

How did Jesus say prayer should be conducted?

What did Jesus say about forgiving others?

How was a fast to be conducted?
Why did Jesus say treasures were to be stored in heaven?

What warning did Jesus give about serving two masters?

What teaching did Jesus give about avoiding anxiety?

Discussion: Why is it so difficult to avoid being anxious?

What teaching did Jesus give about judging and condemning others?

Discussion: Why is it so hard not to judge the behavior of others?

What encouragement did Jesus give to those seeking God's provisions?

What comparison did Jesus make between a wide road and the path chosen by His followers?

How did Jesus say false religious leaders could be spotted?

THE PARABLES OF JESUS
Matthew 8:5–13, 11:2–19, 12:22–13:52
Luke 7:1–8:15, 8:19–21, 11:14–13:21
Mark 3:20–4:32

When you are finished reading this section, you should be able to explain the lessons found in Jesus's parables and explain why He used parables as His primary teaching method.

Describe the centurion from Capernaum.

Why did Jesus heal this man's valuable servant who was deathly ill?

What lesson did Jesus teach by this healing?

What miracle did Jesus perform in Nain?
What reassurance did John the Baptist seek from Jesus?

What evidence did Jesus give to John the Baptist?

What praises did Jesus have for John?

Who approached Jesus while he dined at the house of Simon the Pharisee?

How did this woman treat Jesus?

How did Simon the Pharisee respond?

How did Jesus respond to Simon's thoughts?

How did Jesus respond to the woman?

How did the other guests respond?
Name some of the women who traveled with Jesus and His twelve apostles.

Describe the role of these women.
Who did Jesus heal back in Capernaum?
How did the Pharisees react when they heard about this miracle?

What lesson did Jesus teach about the source of His power?

What sin did Jesus say would not be forgiven?

> *Discussion: Why was this teaching necessary at this time?*

What lesson did Jesus give about spoken words?

What was the "sign of Jonah"?

Describe the historical examples of repentance given by Jesus.

Who did Jesus say was His mother and who were His brothers?

How did Jesus define "inner righteousness"?

What lesson did Jesus teach about hypocrisy?

How did Jesus feel about lawyers who were not helpful?

What warning did Jesus give to His disciples?

Who did Jesus say should not be feared?

Who did Jesus say should be feared instead?

What advice did Jesus give His disciples about defending their faith?

What teaching did Jesus give His disciples about how to handle worry and anxiety?

Review the earlier discussion on why it is so hard to avoid anxiety.

What is the lesson found in Jesus's parable of the watchful servants?

What will be the punishment for the unfaithful believer?

What will be the punishment for the uninformed sinner?

Discussion: Why are the punishments different?

Instead of peace on earth, what did Jesus say was the result of His coming?

What will happen to those who do not repent?

What is the lesson found in Jesus's parable of the unfruitful fig tree?

What miracle did Jesus once again perform on a Sabbath Day?

What was the synagogue ruler's criticism?

How did Jesus handle this attack?

What was the result of Jesus's response?

Why did Jesus say He used parables as a teaching method?

Why didn't everyone understand Jesus's teachings?

Discussion: What keeps us from hearing and understanding the message?

Where was Jesus when He told the parable of the sower?

Recount the parable of the sower.
In this parable, what did the seed represent?

What did the different soils represent?

Recount the parable of the weeds.

In this parable, who was the man that sowed good seed?
What did the field represent?
What did the good seed represent?
What did the weeds represent?
Who sowed the weeds?
What did the harvest represent?
Who were the harvesters?
What will happen to the weeds?

What will happen to the good seed?

What is the message in the parable of the lighted lamp?

What is the lesson in the parable of the growing seed?

What is the lesson in the parable of the mustard seed?

What is the message of the parable of the yeast?

What is the message of the parable of the hidden treasure?

What is the message of the pearl of great price?

What is the lesson in the parable of the net?

What is the message of the parable of treasures?

JESUS'S MIRACLES
Matthew 8:18–34, 9:18–34, 13:53–58
Luke 9:57–62, 8:22–56; Mark 4:35–6:6

> *As you read this section, look for proof that Jesus truly was the Son of God.*

When people said they wanted to follow Jesus, what challenges did they face?

Discussion: What characteristics are required to follow Jesus today?

What happened while Jesus and His disciples were sailing across the Sea of Galilee?

What was Jesus doing during this terrifying event?
What were His disciples doing?
How did Jesus handle this situation?

What did Jesus question?
When Jesus and His disciples reached the region of the Gerasenes (Gadarenes, Gergesenes), what miracle did He perform?

How did the people of this area react when they saw the results of this miracle?

When the healed man asked to go with Jesus, what did Jesus tell him to do instead?

Describe the result of this miracle.
When Jesus and His disciples crossed back over to the other side of the lake, who came to see Jesus?

What did this man want?
As the large crowd pressed in around Jesus, what did He sense?

Who was this person?

Why was this woman healed?
What news came from the house of Jairus?

How did Jesus respond to this news?
Who were the only ones allowed to accompany Jesus?

How did the mourners react when Jesus arrived?

What happened when Jesus took the young girl by the hand?

Describe the reaction of those present.

What strict orders did Jesus give?
Who did Jesus heal next?

What stern warning did Jesus give these two?

Who did Jesus heal next?
Describe the crowd's reaction.
How did the Pharisees respond?

When Jesus returned to His hometown of Nazareth, how was His teaching in the synagogue received?

Why wasn't Jesus's ministry very effective here?

APOSTLES ARE SENT OUT
Matthew 9:35–11:1, 14:1–13; Mark 6:6–33; Luke 9:1–11; John 6:1

As Jesus traveled around teaching, preaching, and healing, what problem did He see?

What was His solution?

Discussion: Why do you think Jesus sent the apostles out in pairs?

What specific instructions did Jesus give these men?

What warnings did Jesus give them?

Discussion: Do any of these warnings apply to believers today?

What was the significance of Jesus using the phrase "anyone who does not take his cross and follow me is not worthy of me. Whoever finds his life will lose it, and whoever loses his life for my sake will find it." (Matthew 10:38–39)

Where did Jesus and His apostles go next?

As word about Jesus's ministry reached King Herod, what was Herod's reaction?

Why were Herod and Herodias so angry with John the Baptist?

Why was Herod willing to imprison John but reluctant to have him killed?

How did Herodias scheme to cause John's death?

Why did Jesus and the apostles sail to the far shore of the Sea of Galilee?

JESUS AND THE MULTITUDES
(April, 29 AD)
Matthew 14:14–16:12; Mark 6:34–8:26
Luke 9:11–17; John 6:2–7:1

As you read this section, look for more evidence of the deity of Jesus and of His great love for all people.

When Jesus arrived on shore, what did He find?

What problem arose?

How did Jesus solve this problem?

What was the result of this miracle?

How did Jesus handle this situation?

What happened to the disciples while crossing the lake?

What did Jesus do when He saw how His disciples were struggling?

How did His disciples react?
What was Peter's response when Jesus identified Himself?

What happened when Peter left the boat?

What happened when both men climbed into the boat?
How was the disciples' reaction to this miracle different from their reaction to the feeding of the five thousand?

What happened when they landed at Gennesaret?

When the crowd from the opposite side of the lake arrived and questioned Jesus about the works of God, what was His answer?
They said Moses had miraculously given the Israelites manna in the desert. What miracle was Jesus prepared to perform to prove He had been sent by God?

How did the Jews respond to Jesus's claim?

What hard teaching did Jesus give about being the bread of life?

What was the result of this difficult message?

Who represented the feelings of the Twelve?
Where did they stand?

Which of the Twelve was a "devil"?
Why did the Pharisees and some teachers of the law condemn some of Jesus's disciples?

How did Jesus respond to this criticism?

What lesson did Jesus give on "cleanliness"?

Why did Jesus minister only in Galilee?

(Go to https://theologue.wordpress.com/2014/04/30/zaine-ridling-bible-atlas-e-book/. Use Map 109, "The Ministry of Jesus Beyond Galilee," to track Jesus' travels after He left Galilee.)

Where did Jesus and His disciples go next?

Who came to see Jesus? Why?
At first, why didn't Jesus respond to this woman's request?

What did this woman say to convince Jesus to help her?

Where did Jesus go next?

Who did Jesus heal here? How?

What was the result of this miracle?

What situation occurred again?

How did Jesus solve this problem?

How many were fed?
Where did Jesus go next?

Who showed up to test Jesus again?

How did Jesus answer these people?

After sailing away from this area, what teaching did Jesus give to His disciples?

Where did Jesus and His disciples go next?
Who was healed here? How?

Why did Jesus keep taking the sick off by themselves for healing followed by a request not to tell what had happened to them?

PREPARING THE APOSTLES FOR THE END
Matthew 16:13–18:35; Mark 8:27–9:50; Luke 9:18–50, 17:1–10

Where did the disciples and Jesus go next?
What question arose?
What possible answers were given?
What answer did Peter give?
What was the significance of Peter's answer?

What future sufferings did Jesus say He must endure?

How did Peter respond to these predictions?

How did Jesus respond to Peter?

What teaching did Jesus give about the cost of discipleship?

Discussion: What is the "cost of discipleship" today?

What happened six days later?

Who was with Jesus during this amazing event?
Describe their location.
How did these men react to what they were seeing?

When the group returned from this event, what was taking place?

What did the boy's father ask of Jesus?

How did Jesus respond?

How much faith did Jesus say it took to move a mountain?

When they reached Capernaum, what did the tax collectors want?

How did Peter get the required payment?

What had the apostles been arguing about on their way to Capernaum?

What teaching did Jesus give them?

How did Jesus feel about children?

How did Jesus feel about "lost sheep" and little ones?

What warning did Jesus give about temptation?

What teaching did Jesus give on how to deal with a brother who sins against another brother?

What teaching did Jesus give about the power of agreement?

What teaching did Jesus give Peter about forgiveness?

Recount the parable of the servants in debt. Explain the message found in this parable.

RETURN TO JERUSALEM FOR
FEAST OF TABERNACLES
(Capernaum, Late September/Early October, 29 AD)
John 7:2–10:21

What was celebrated at the Feast of the Tabernacles?

Why did Jesus's brothers want Him to attend this feast?

Why did Jesus refuse to go with them?

(Jerusalem, October, 29 AD)

In what manner did Jesus travel to Jerusalem to attend this feast?

Describe the reaction Jesus was getting from the Jews at this time.

On the last day of the feast, what teaching did Jesus give about "living water"?

Why didn't the temple guards arrest Jesus?
Who cautioned the Pharisees and chief priests against condemning Jesus without due process?

The next day while Jesus was teaching in the temple courts, what trap was set?

How did Jesus handle this situation?

Explain how Jesus is the "light of the world."

Even though His words angered the Pharisees, why wasn't Jesus arrested?

What did Jesus say would happen to those who did not believe He was the Son of God?

When would everyone finally believe who Jesus really was?

How would Jesus's disciples be recognizable?

Discussion: What makes the followers of Jesus recognizable today?

How did Jesus describe the devil?

Jesus said anyone who kept His word would never die. How is this possible?

How did Jesus know Abraham had rejoiced at the thought of seeing His work on earth even though they lived two thousand years apart?
How did the Jews react to this information?

Why did Jesus's disciples think a certain man was blind from birth?

Why did Jesus say the man was blind?
What did Jesus tell the man to do to be healed?

Why did the Pharisees have a problem with this healing?

When questioned by the Pharisees, who did the healed man say Jesus was?
Who did the blind man's parents say had healed their son?

When questioned again, what was the healed man's response?

After the Jews threw him out of the synagogue and Jesus confronted him, how did the healed man respond?

Explain the message Jesus was trying to convey in the story of the sheep and their shepherd.

How were the Jews still reacting to Jesus?

JESUS'S MINISTRY FROM GALILEE TO JUDEA
(Capernaum, Galilee)
Matthew 19:1–2, 11:20–30; Mark 10:1
Luke 9:51–56, 17:11–19, 10:1–11:13

> *As you read this section, take note of the teachings
> emphasized by Jesus during His final days on earth.*

(Go to https://theologue.wordpress.com/2014/04/30/zaine-ridling-bible-atlas-e-book/. Use Map 110, "Jesus's Journeys from Galilee to Judea," to track the final stages of His ministry.)

What route did Jesus take on His way to Jerusalem?

How did the people in this region treat Jesus?
What group of men called out to Jesus for healing?
What did Jesus tell them to do?

How did these men respond?

Who did Jesus commission to help spread the word of God?

What kind of response did these men get?

Of what did Jesus remind them?

What did Jesus promise for the weary and burdened?

Discussion: What is so comforting about these verses?

What question did the expert in the law ask Jesus?
How did Jesus answer this question?

How did the lawyer answer the question asked by Jesus?

What was the lawyer's next question?

Recount the parable of the Good Samaritan.

Who was the neighbor in the parable?
What advice did Jesus give to the lawyer?

Who offered hospitality to Jesus and His disciples as they traveled to Jerusalem?

What problem arose?

How did Jesus respond when Martha asked for help?

What did Jesus teach His disciples to do?

What teaching did Jesus give using the parable of persistence?

What teaching did Jesus give about the proper prayer attitude?

BACK IN JERUSALEM FOR FEAST OF DEDICATION
(Jerusalem, November/December, 29 AD)
John 10:22–42

As you read this section, look for an escalation in the plot to kill Jesus.

What was the Feast of Dedication?

As Jesus was walking into the temple, what did the Jews ask Him?
How did Jesus answer them?

Why did the Jews want to stone Jesus?

After escaping, where did Jesus go next?

JESUS'S MINISTRY IN PEREA
Luke 13:22–16:31, 17:20–18:14; Matthew 20:1–16

Who ruled this area?

How did Jesus respond when asked if only a few would be saved?

Who came to give Jesus a warning?
What was the warning?
How did Jesus respond?

How did Jesus feel about the people of Jerusalem?

One Sabbath, who hosted Jesus for a meal?
What issue came up again?
What did Jesus do to prove His point?

What teaching did Jesus give about choosing seats at a feast?

Who should be invited?

Explain Jesus's message in the parable of the great banquet.

What did Jesus say was the cost of following Him?

Explain Jesus's teaching in the parable of the salt.

What are the lessons of the lost sheep, lost coin, and lost son?

Explain Jesus's message in the parable of the dishonest manager.

What did Jesus know about the hearts of the Pharisees?

Recount the story of the rich man and Lazarus.

What lessons are found in this story?

When did Jesus say the kingdom of God would come?

When will Jesus come again?

Explain Jesus's message in the parable of the persistent widow.

Explain Jesus's message in the parable of the Pharisee and the tax collector.

How did Jesus say the kingdom of heaven was like a man who owned a vineyard?

JESUS RAISES LAZARUS FROM THE DEAD
John 11:1–54

(Go to https://theologue.wordpress.com/2014/04/30/zaine-ridling-bible-atlas-e-book/. Use Map 111, "Jesus in Judea and Jerusalem," to follow Jesus on the final days of His ministry.)

Where was Jesus?
Who was Lazarus?
Where did Lazarus live?
What was wrong with Lazarus?

How did Jesus respond when He heard about Lazarus?

Why did His disciples discourage Jesus from returning to Judea?

What did Jesus know about Lazarus that His disciples did not?

What did Thomas think was going to happen?
Where was Lazarus when Jesus arrived?
When Martha went out to meet Jesus, what did she tell Him?

What did Jesus tell Martha?
What did Martha think Jesus meant?

What truth did Jesus share with Martha?

When Mary also left Bethany to meet Jesus, who followed her?
How did Jesus react when he saw Mary and those with her?

What did Jesus do next?

Discussion: How was the resurrection of Lazarus different from the resurrections of the widow's son and Jairus's daughter?

How did those who witnessed this miracle respond?

What did the chief priests and the Pharisees do?

Who was the high priest?
What had he prophesied?

How did the outcome of this meeting affect Jesus?

JESUS'S FINAL JOURNEY
(January–March, 30 AD)
Matthew 19:3–30, 20:17–34, 26:6–13
Mark 10:2–52, 14:3–9
Luke 18:15–19:28
John 11:55–12:11

The plot thickens ...

Why did the Pharisees ask Jesus about divorce?

What was Jesus's answer?

Who were people bringing to be blessed by Jesus?
Why did Jesus say the kingdom of God belonged to individuals like these?

What question did the rich young man have for Jesus?
How did Jesus answer him?

How did the rich young man respond?

Why did Jesus say it was hard for the rich to enter heaven?

What did Jesus say His disciples would receive as a result of their sacrifice?

On His way to Jerusalem with His disciples, what did Jesus predict?

How did His disciples react to this information?

What did James and John and their mother want from Jesus?

What did Jesus tell them?

When the other disciples became upset with this request, what lesson did Jesus teach them?

Where did Jesus go next?

Who was Zacchaeus?
What did he do to get a glimpse of Jesus?

What did Jesus say when He saw Zacchaeus?
Why did the other people present have a problem with this?

What promise did Zacchaeus make?

How did Jesus justify his relationship with Zacchaeus?

On their way out of Jericho, who did Jesus and His disciples see?

What was this man shouting?
What did he want from Jesus?
What did Jesus do?

What was the result of this miracle?

As the travel party neared Jerusalem, why did Jesus tell the parable of the ten minas?

What was a "mina"?
Who was the "man of noble birth" in this story?

In this story, how did the king deal with each of the three servants?

Why were so many people traveling to Jerusalem at this time?

Why were the Jews in the temple area looking for Jesus?

Where was Jesus?

Who else was there? Describe what each person was doing.

Who had a problem with Mary's actions? Why?

What did Jesus say was the intended purpose of the perfume?

How would Mary be remembered?

Why had a large crowd of Jews come to Bethany?

Triumphant Entry into Jerusalem
(Sunday, Late March, 30 AD)
John 12:12–19; Matthew 21:1–11, 17
Mark 11:1–11; Luke 19:29–44

> *As you read about the last week of Jesus's life on earth, look for the fulfillment of the prophecies about the Messiah, God's own Son.*

(Go to https://theologue.wordpress.com/2014/04/30/zaine-ridling-bible-atlas-e-book/. Use Map 112, "Jerusalem in the New Testament Period," to locate the places mentioned in this section.)

What was commemorated at the Feast of the Passover?

Discussion: How is Jesus about to become the "Lamb that was slain"?

How did the crowd greet Jesus?

As Jesus approached Bethphage and Bethany at the Mount of Olives, what did He tell two of His disciples to obtain in the village?

Why did Jesus need this animal?

What happened when Jesus entered Jerusalem?

Why did Jesus weep over the city of Jerusalem?

How did the people respond to seeing Jesus?

How did the Pharisees respond?

After visiting the temple, why didn't Jesus stay in the city?

(Monday)
Matthew 21: 12-19; Mark 11: 12-19; Luke 19: 45-48; John 12: 20-36

What did Jesus do to the unfruitful fig tree?

When Jesus reached the temple in Jerusalem, what did He do?

Why did Jesus do this?

Why didn't the chief priests and teachers of the law immediately arrest Jesus and have Him killed?

Where did the phrase "out of the mouth of babes" originate?

To what did Jesus compare His death?

What did Jesus say was the purpose of His death?

How did Jesus feel about fulfilling His mission?

What did God do to encourage Jesus?

What did Jesus say would be accomplished by His death?

How did Jesus say He would die?
Where did Jesus go at the end of the day?
Explain how Jesus could remain forever if He was going to die.

Explain Jesus's teaching about walking in light or darkness.

(Tuesday Morning)
Matthew 21:20–23:39; Mark 11:20–12:44; Luke 20:1–21:4
Matthew 24:1–25:46; Mark 13:1–37; Luke 21:5–36

As they returned to Jerusalem, what lessons on faith, belief, and forgiveness did Jesus teach using the cursed fig tree?

When Jesus's authority was questioned, how did He respond?

Why were the questioners caught?

What answer did the questioners give?
In the parable of the two sons, what group did the first son represent? What group did the second son represent?

Explain the message of this parable.

Who were the tenants in the parable of the murderous tenants?

Explain the message of this parable.

How did the "murderous tenants" react to this parable?

In the parable of the wedding banquet, what did the banquet represent?
Who was the king?
Who was the son?
Who were the servants?
Who were the first invited guests? What happened to them?

Who were the second invited guests?
Who was the improperly dressed man?

What happened to this man?

Who did the Pharisees send to try to trap Jesus again?

What was the trick question this time?

212

How did Jesus handle this tricky situation?

Describe the effect of Jesus's answer.
Who questioned Jesus next?
What was their question?

How did Jesus answer them?

Describe the effect of Jesus's answer.
What question was asked by one of the teachers of the law?

How did Jesus answer?

Discuss the importance of being obedient to this "greatest command."

What question did Jesus have for the Pharisees?
How did they answer?
Why did Jesus think this answer was incorrect?

What effect did Jesus's answer have on the crowd?

What problems did Jesus have with the Pharisees and teachers of the law?

List the seven woes Jesus presented to these religious leaders.

Discussion: Considering these woes, what characteristics do you think are most important to God?

How did Jesus feel about the inhabitants of Jerusalem? Why?

Why did Jesus make an example of the widow's offering?

What prediction did Jesus make about the temple?

What three questions did Peter, James, John, and Andrew privately ask Jesus?

What did Jesus tell theses four apostles?

What did Jesus say would happen when the end came?

How did Jesus say He would come again?

When did Jesus say He would come again?

Explain Jesus's message in the parable of the wise and foolish virgins.

Explain Jesus's message in the parable of the talents.

How did Jesus describe the last judgment?

(Tuesday Afternoon)
Matthew 26:1–5, 14–16; Mark 14:1–2, 10–11; Luke 22:1–6

How many days was it before the Passover was to take place?
What was going to happen then?
What were the chief priests and Jewish elders doing?

Why did they want to get the deed done before the Passover?
Who became a fellow conspirator?

What was the going price for this betrayal?

Luke 21:37–38, 22:7–13; John 12:37–50; Matthew 26:17–19; Mark 14:12–16

On what day was Passover observed?
What feast followed Passover?

What event did this feast commemorate?

What was the main course for the Passover meal?

How was Jesus spending His last days and nights?

Describe how the people were being affected by Jesus's messages.

Discussion: Is the effect of the gospel message on people any different today?

Describe the final public appeal made by Jesus.

What did Jesus send Peter and John to do?
How would Peter and John know where to go?

The Last Supper
Luke 22:14–39; Matthew 26:20–35
Mark 14:17–31; John 13:1–14:31

As you read about the Last Supper, look for a new memorial, a new command, and the promise of a new manifestation of a spiritual entity.

Why was this occasion so important?

What new memorial did Jesus institute?

What clue did Jesus give about His betrayer?

What dispute arose among the apostles?

What didn't the apostles understand?

After the evening meal was served, what act did Jesus perform? Why?

Who refused this humble act?

How did Jesus respond?

What additional clues did Jesus give about His betrayer?

Who was the betrayer?
Whose influence was this man under? Why?

What new command did Jesus give?
What was the purpose of this new command?

What question did Peter ask Jesus?
How did Jesus answer?

What did Peter offer to do for Jesus?

What did Jesus predict Peter would do?

Where did Jesus say He was going?

What question did Thomas ask Jesus?

How did Jesus answer?

What did Jesus say people would do if they loved Him?
Who did Jesus promise to send as a counselor for His disciples?

Describe the role of this "counselor."

What comfort did Jesus leave with His disciples?

Whose command was Jesus under? Why?

Where did Jesus and His apostles go next?
What prediction did Jesus make about how His apostles would react when the "shepherd" was struck down?

Final Teachings to His Disciples
John 15:1–17:26

Describe how Jesus used a vine and its branches to teach His disciples a lesson about fruitfulness.

What was to be the end result of "bearing fruit"?

What command did Jesus give about how to love?

Why did Jesus say the world would hate His disciples?

Why did Jesus say His disciples would face persecution?

Discussion: What examples of Christian persecution do you see in the world today?

What had to happen before the counselor could come?

What did Jesus say that really had the disciples confused?

What was the key to understanding what Jesus said?

In His prayer, why did Jesus say God granted Him authority over all people?

Explain what this means.

When was Jesus first with God?
What did Jesus pray for God to provide to His eleven apostles?

What did Jesus pray for God to provide to all believers?

When did God first develop His plan of salvation?

Jesus's Betrayal and Arrest

(Wednesday Night)

Matthew 26:36–56; Mark 14:32–52; Luke 22:40–53; John 18:1–12

Where did Jesus and His disciples go next?

What did Jesus ask His disciples to do?
Who did Jesus take aside?
What was Jesus feeling at this time?

What did Jesus ask these three to do?
Where did Jesus go?
What was Jesus's prayer?

Who appeared? Why?

Describe the state Jesus was in during His second prayer time.

When Jesus went back to His three disciples, what were they doing?

What did Jesus tell Peter?

What was Jesus's prayer the second time?

What were His three disciples doing when Jesus returned this time?
What did Jesus do next?

What were Peter, James, and John doing the third time Jesus returned?

What was about to happen?
Who showed up?

Describe the betrayal signal given to Jesus's captors.

> *Discuss the significance of this action as a sign of betrayal.*

How many disciples were killed in this altercation?

What did Peter do when Jesus was seized?

How did Jesus respond?

How did His followers respond when Jesus was arrested?

Jesus's Trial before the Sanhedrin

(Jerusalem, 30 AD)

John 18: 12-27; Matthew 26: 57-27:10; Mark 14: 53-15: 1; Luke 22: 40-53

Where did His captors take Jesus?

Who was the guard on the door to the high priest's courtyard?
What question did this person ask Peter?

How did Peter answer her?
Why was Jesus brought before this high priest?

Where was Jesus taken next?
Where was Peter?
Who recognized him?

How did Peter react this time?

Who met to falsely accuse Jesus?

How did Jesus respond?
When He was asked if He was the Christ, the Son of the Blessed One, how did Jesus answer?

Based on His answer, what was the crime?
What was the penalty for this crime?

Describe what happened to Jesus next.

A little while later, what gave away Peter's association with Jesus?

How did Peter respond when challenged about his relationship with Jesus?

What happened as Peter was responding to this third challenge?

Describe Peter's reaction.
Where was Jesus at daybreak?

What did this group want to know?

How did Jesus answer them?
Based on His answer, what decision did this group make?

How did Judas react to this verdict?

What happened to the money Judas had accepted?

Jesus's Trial before Pilate
(April, 30 AD)
Matthew 27:2, 11–32; Mark 15:1–22; Luke 23:1–31; John 18:28–19:17

Where was Jesus taken next?

Why was Jesus taken before this man?

Why couldn't the Jews enter the palace (Praetorium)?

What question did this man ask Jesus?
How did Jesus respond?

What did this man decide to do with Jesus?

How did this man and his soldiers treat Jesus?

What warning did the governor's wife have for her husband?

At this point, what justification was there for the charges against Jesus?

What punishment did Pilate recommend?
What custom was performed at the Feast of Unleavened Bread?

What was Pilate's suggestion? Why?

Who did the Jews want instead?
What did the Jews demand?

What did Pilate do in the face of their demand?

Why did Pilate become frustrated with Jesus?

What statement did Jesus finally make about who was in control?

When Pilate tried to step away from this situation one last time, what did the Jews question?

What day was it?
What did Pilate finally do? Why?

When the Jews finally got control of Jesus, what did they do?

Who did the Jews force to help carry the cross?

Where were they taking Jesus?

Jesus's Crucifixion
(9 am–Noon)
Matthew 27:33–56; Mark 15:23–41
Luke 23:32–49; John 19:18–37

As you read this section, think about the sacrifice made by Jesus, why He had to die, and for whom he died. Take note of how the heart-wrenching treatment of Jesus resulted in the glorious fulfillment of the Messianic prophecies and in the establishment of a new covenant relationship between the human race and Almighty God.

At what time was Jesus crucified?
What were Jesus's first words from the cross?

What drink was offered to Jesus?

Who else was being crucified with Jesus?
What was the inscription fastened to Jesus's cross?

Who prepared this sign?
What happened to Jesus's clothes? Why?

How did the crowd react to seeing Jesus on the cross?

What drink did the soldiers offer to Jesus?
How did one of the crucified criminals insult Jesus?

How did the other crucified criminal react to this insult?

What was Jesus's promise to this criminal?
Identify the women at the cross.

Who did Jesus ask to take care of His mother?
What happened between the sixth (noon) and ninth (three pm) hours?

What did Jesus cry out?
What did Jesus request? What was He given?

What were Jesus's last words as He hung on the cross?

What happened at that very moment?

Describe how these events affected those who were watching.

What day was it?
Why did the Jews ask Pilate to break the legs of the crucified?

Why were Jesus's legs not broken?

What did the soldier do to make sure Jesus was dead?

Jesus's Burial
(Garden near Golgotha)
Matthew 27:57–66; Mark 15:42–47; Luke 23:50–56; John 19:38–42

Who came to Pilate and asked for Jesus's body?

Why did this request surprise Pilate?
Who assisted in Jesus's burial?

What did this man bring?
How was Jesus's body prepared for burial?

Where was Jesus buried?

Why didn't the women who followed Jesus immediately anoint His body?

What did the chief priests and Pharisees ask Pilate to do? Why?

How was this accomplished?

Jesus's Resurrection
(Sunday Morning to Sunday Evening, at the Tomb and on the Road to Emmaus)
Matthew 28:1–15; Mark 16:1–14
Luke 24:1–44; John 20:1–21:24

How was the tomb opened?

How did the soldiers who were guarding the tomb react?

Just after sunrise on Sunday morning, who went to the tomb? Why?

Who did these women see when they entered the tomb area?

What were they told?
Who else appeared?
What was their message?

How did the women react to what they saw and heard?
What did Mary Magdalene tell Peter and John?

How did Peter and John react to this information?

Who was the first person to see Jesus after His resurrection?

Who did she think He was?
How did she know this man was Jesus?
What was her immediate reaction?

What did Jesus tell her to do?

How did the women feel after seeing Jesus?
How did the chief priests react when the guards told them Jesus's tomb was empty?

How did the eleven disciples react when the women told them Jesus's tomb was empty?

Who was walking on the road to Emmaus?
What did Jesus ask them?
What was their reaction to His question?

What was their topic of discussion?

How did Jesus reveal His identity to these two men?

What did these two men do?

Who appeared while their report was being given?
How did the disciples react?

How did Jesus reassure them?

What authority did Jesus give the eleven? How?

What proof did Thomas require before he would believe Jesus had truly risen?

Describe what happened one week later.

Recount what happened when Jesus appeared to His disciples for the third time.

Describe the conversation Jesus had with Peter after breakfast.

What did Jesus foretell about Peter?

What did Peter want to know about John?

How did Jesus answer?

Jesus's Final Instructions and His Ascension
(On a Mountain in Galilee and in Jerusalem before Pentecost)
Matthew 28:16–20; Mark 16:15–20; Luke 24:45–53; John 20:30–31, 21:25; Acts 1:6–26

Where were Jesus and the eleven?

What great commission did Jesus give to the apostles?

Who did Jesus say would be saved?

How would the world know the apostles acted in Jesus's name?

What did Jesus tell them they would receive?

Where did Jesus and the eleven go next?

After being blessed by Jesus, what question did they have?

How did Jesus answer?

What happened to Jesus?

Who appeared and what did they want to know?

What message did they have?

What did the apostles do next?

Identify those in this group.

How many believers were present at this time?

Who was chosen to replace Judas Iscariot?

What was the purpose of recording the events of Jesus's life, death, and resurrection?

The Establishment of a New Body of Believers: The Beginning of Christianity

(30–100 AD)

After reading this section, you should be able to describe how Christ's church was established, explain how the gospel message was spread, and give examples that prove salvation is for all.

ACTS OF CHRIST'S APOSTLES
(Jerusalem, 30–31 AD)
Acts 1:1–5, 2:1–6:7

Who wrote the Acts of the Apostles?

Who was the recipient of this letter?

How long was Jesus on earth after His resurrection and before His ascension?
What was He doing during this time?

What feast was being celebrated?
What happened to the apostles on this day?

Who came to see what was happening?

Why were these people amazed?
What did the scoffers think?
Who stood up to speak?
How did this man respond to the scoffers?

What evidence did Peter give to confirm Jesus was from God?

Who did Peter say was responsible for Jesus's death on the cross?

Why did God allow Jesus to be handed over to those who would kill Him?

226

How did God free Jesus from death?

Why did Peter's words cut this audience to the heart?

What did these people want to know?

What did they need to do?

What would they receive?

Describe this audience's response to Peter's sermon on this day.

Discussion: What should everyone's response be to the gospel message today?

Describe the actions of this growing group of believers.

Where were Peter and John headed?
Who did they meet?

What did this man want?
What did Peter give him instead?
Describe the result of Peter's actions.

What important message did Peter preach?

What happened to Peter and John as a result of their preaching?

How did the crowd respond to Peter and John's message?

Where were Peter and John taken the next day?

What did this group want to know?
What explanation did Peter give for his actions?

Why were Peter and John just warned and released?

How did Peter and John respond to the warning?

How did God answer the church's prayer for boldness to preach the word?

Describe how the early church's physical needs were met.

Describe someone who was a good example of this.

Describe a couple who were bad examples.

What effect did this event have on the church?

Where did the church meet?

Why were some afraid to join the church?

> *Discussion: Do we face similar fears today?*

How did people demonstrate their faith in Peter's power to heal?

Who imprisoned the apostles? Why?

How did the apostles escape?

What happened when the Sanhedrin sent for the prisoners?

Where were the prisoners?

Why didn't the captain and his officers use force to bring the apostles before the Sanhedrin?

What was the Sanhedrin's complaint?

How did Peter and the other apostles respond?

How did the Sanhedrin respond?

Who prevented the apostles from being harmed? How?

What did the Sanhedrin do to the apostles?

How did the apostles respond to this punishment?

What problem arose among the disciples?

How was this problem handled?

Who was chosen for this service?

Describe the growth of the church at this time.

STEPHEN'S MARTYRDOM
Acts 6:8–8:1

As you read this section, look for the qualities found in a true martyr and be able to describe the effects of martyrdom.

Who was Stephen?

Who was upset with Stephen?

Why were these people so frustrated with Stephen?

What tactic did they employ to convict Stephen before the Sanhedrin?

Describe Stephen's face during his trial.

What was Stephen's defense?

How did the members of the Sanhedrin respond?

Who did Stephen say he saw?

Describe the reaction of the Sanhedrin.

At whose feet did the witnesses place their clothes?

What were this first martyr's last words?

PERSECUTION AS THE GOSPEL IS SPREAD

(Jerusalem, Samaria
Road to Gaza and Caesarea)
Acts 8:1–40

After reading this section, you should be able to give examples of Christian persecution as well as describe how God used this harassment.

(Go to https://theologue.wordpress.com/2014/04/30/zaine-ridling-bible-atlas-e-book/. Use Map 117, "Expansion of the Early Church in Palestine," to follow the apostles as they spread the gospel message.)

What happened to the church after the stoning of Stephen?

Who was fervently involved in this persecution?
What was this man doing to believers?

Once they were scattered, what were the believers doing?

Where did Philip go?
What did Philip do here?

Who was one of Philip's converts?
Who did the apostles send from Jerusalem to Samaria?

What did these men do for the new converts?

When Simon saw Peter and John's special power, what did he want?

How did Simon intend to get what he wanted?

How did Simon respond when rebuked by Peter?

Why did Philip go down the road that led from Jerusalem to Gaza?

Who did Philip meet?

What was this man doing?

Why did Philip approach the chariot?
What did Philip ask this man?
How did this man answer?
What explanation did this man want?
What did Philip tell him?
Describe the result of Philip's message.

What happened to Philip when they came up out of the water?

SAUL'S CONVERSION
(Near Damascus, Syria)
(35 AD)
Acts 9:1–31

Where was Saul going? Why?

As he neared his destination, who spoke to Saul?

What question was asked of Saul?
What did the voice tell Saul to do?
Describe Saul's physical condition following this event.

Who was Ananias?
Who spoke to Ananias in a vision?
What request was made of Ananias?

Why was Ananias reluctant to go?

How was Ananias reassured?

What happened when Ananias went to see Saul?

What was Saul's first order of business?

Why were people astonished?

How did the Jews feel about Saul's conversion?

How was their plan defeated?

Where did Saul go?
Why were the disciples here afraid of Saul?

Who stood up for Saul?
What did Saul do in this city?
Why did Saul have to leave?
Where did Saul go next?

Describe the growth of the church at this time.

FIRST GENTILE FOLLOWERS
(Lydda, Sharon, Joppa, Caesarea,
Jerusalem, Antioch)
Acts 9:32–11:30

As you read this section, look for teachings about how the old law and temple worship have been replaced by a new covenant and a new way to worship. You should be able to describe this new covenant and explain how worship has changed.

Where did Peter go?

Who did Peter heal here?

Describe the effect of this miracle.

Where did Peter go next?

Why did Peter go to this town?

What did Peter do when he arrived?
Who was Cornelius?

Who did Cornelius see in a vision?
Describe the message.

Describe the vision Peter had at about noon the next day.

Why was this request a problem for Peter?

What command was given to Peter?

How many times was this scene repeated?
Who arrived at Simon's house?

How did Peter know it was okay to go with these men?

What happened when Peter arrived in Caesarea?

What message did Peter have for these Gentiles?

While Peter was speaking, what happened to these Gentiles?

Why was this so strange?

What did Peter say these Gentiles had to be allowed to do?

When Peter went to Jerusalem, what criticism did he face?

How did Peter respond to this criticism?

How did his critics respond after they heard Peter's story?

What effect did Stephen's martyrdom have on the spread of the gospel?

How did the Greeks in Antioch hear the good news about Jesus?

Who did the church in Jerusalem send to Antioch? Why?

Why did this man go to Tarsus?
What did these two men do in Antioch?

What name was first given to the followers of Jesus at Antioch?
Who predicted a severe famine would affect the entire Roman world?

What gift was taken back to Jerusalem?

MORE PERSECUTION
(Jerusalem, Caesarea, and Antioch)
Acts 12:1–25

Who was the current ruler of the Roman Empire?

What did this king begin to do?
Who did he put to death by the sword?
Who else was arrested and put in prison?
What feast was being celebrated?
How many soldiers were assigned to guard this prisoner?
How did the church respond to this man's imprisonment?

What happened the night before the trial was to begin?

Where did Peter go?

What were the Christians gathered here doing?

Who came to the door?
What was her response?

What did the people gathered there think?

What happened to the prison guards?
What happened to Herod Agrippa in Caesarea?

Who accompanied Barnabas and Saul to Jerusalem?

Paul's Journeys and Letters

(46–67 AD)

PAUL'S FIRST MISSIONARY JOURNEY
(46–47 AD)
Acts 13:1–14:28

(Go to https://theologue.wordpress.com/2014/04/30/zaine-ridling-bible-atlas-e-book/. Use Map 119, "The First Missionary Journey of Paul," to follow Paul's travels as he preaches the gospel.)

Who was working in the church at Antioch at this time?

Who did the Holy Spirit set apart for a special ministry?
Where did their journey begin?

Who went with them?
Who did they meet at Paphos?

What was this man trying to do?

What was Saul's new name?

What did Paul do to this "child of the devil"?

What effect did this action have on the proconsul?
Where did the three missionaries go next?

Who left the group and returned to Jerusalem?
Where did Paul and Barnabas go next?
Who gave his first recorded sermon in the synagogue on the Sabbath?
Describe Paul's audience.
What was Paul's message?

How did the people of this city respond to Paul's message?

How did the local Jews feel about the people's response?

What effect did this attitude have on the spread of the gospel?

What action did the Jews take next?

How did Paul and Barnabas respond?

Where did they go next?
What did they do here?

Describe this audience's response to the gospel message.

What plot was stirring?
How was this persecution avoided?
Where did Paul and Barnabas go next?

What miracle occurred in Lystra?

How did the crowd think Paul was able to perform this miracle?

How did Paul and Barnabas feel about the crowd's intentions?

Who came from Antioch and Iconium?

What did they do to Paul?

Where did Paul and Barnabas go next?
Describe the response to the good news here.
Where did Paul and Barnabas go next? Why?

What did the two missionaries do once they returned to Antioch?

THE JERUSALEM CONFERENCE
(Antioch, Syria, Jerusalem)
(48–50 AD)
Acts 15:1–35

What issue prompted the Jerusalem Conference?

Who addressed this issue before the apostles and elders?
What points did Peter make regarding this issue?

Who presented a workable solution?

Describe his proposal.

What disclaimer was in the opening of the letter?

Who carried the letter to the Gentile believers?

How did the Gentile believers respond when the letter was read?

Who stayed to continue teaching and preaching the Word?

PAUL'S LETTER TO THE GALATIANS
(50–52 AD)
The Book of Galatians

> *As you read this letter, look for answers to the question of Gentile circumcision, believer's justification, and attainment of salvation, which comes by way of a new covenant relationship with God through faith in Jesus and is made possible by God's grace and not by strict adherence to the law. You should be able to explain how the law is truly fulfilled.*

Who wrote the letter to the Galatians?
To whom was the letter written?

Who did the writer say commissioned him to deliver the gospel?

What was already happening in these churches?

What did the writer say would happen to anyone who preached a gospel other than the true one?

Describe the writer's background and authority to teach about Jesus.

Why did Paul rebuke the apostle Peter?

What did Paul say did *not* justify believers?

How are believers justified?

Could the goal (of salvation) be attained by human effort? How is salvation attained?

How did the faith of Abraham, the father of Israel, affect all Gentiles?

How did Christ redeem believers from the curse of trying to keep the old law?

Describe how God's covenant is based on His promise and not on the Law of Moses.

What was the purpose of the law?
How do all believers become sons of God and heirs to the promise?

Why was Paul so distressed over these Christians?

In Paul's allegory, what do Hagar and her son, Ishmael, represent?

What do Sarah and Isaac represent?

What did Paul say would happen if these Gentile men were circumcised just to fulfill Jewish law?

How is the law truly fulfilled?

What two aspects are found in every person?
How are these in conflict with each other?

Make a list of some of the acts of the sinful nature.

What warning did Paul give to those who live by their sinful nature?

Make a list of characteristics produced as a result of living by the Spirit.

What have those who belong to Christ done to their sinful nature?

What responsibility do brothers have to one another?

What does the man who lives to please his sinful nature get?

What does the man who lives to please the Spirit get?
Why did Paul say the Judaizers were compelling the Gentile believers to be circumcised?

What was the only thing about which a believer should ever brag?

PAUL'S SECOND MISSIONARY JOURNEY

(49/50–52 AD)

Acts 15:36–18:11

> *As you read this section, look for similarities between Paul's first missionary journey and this one, i.e., common message, problems, and persecutions.*

(Go to https://theologue.wordpress.com/2014/04/30/zaine-ridling-bible-atlas-e-book/. Use Map 120, "The Second Missionary Journey of Paul," to follow Paul's travels as he preaches the gospel to Greece and back.)

Where was Paul at this time?
What did Paul want to do?

What dispute arose between Paul and Barnabas?

How was this disagreement settled?

Who did Paul and Silas meet in Lystra?
Describe this man.

Name the towns these men traveled through after leaving Lystra.
What happened when they reached the border of Mysia and Bithynia?

Where did they go next?
What happened to Paul here?

Where did they go next?

Who did they meet by the river outside this city?

Describe this woman's response to Paul's message.

On the way to their place of prayer one day, who did they meet?

What did Paul do for this girl?

Why did this simple act of compassion create such a major problem?

What happened to Paul and Silas as a result of their actions?

What charge was leveled against Paul and Silas?

Describe Paul and Silas's punishment.

What happened about midnight that night?

What did the jailer do when he woke up?

What stopped the jailer from completing his intended action?

How did the jailer respond?

What did Paul and Silas tell the jailer?

What was the result of their message?

Even though officers of the court brought word the next morning that Paul and Silas were to be released, why did Paul have a problem with the way they had been treated?

How did the magistrates respond?

Where did Paul and Silas go instead?
After leaving Philippi, where did Paul and Silas go next?

What did Paul do when their group reached Thessalonica?

Describe the result of Paul's efforts.

What did the jealous Jews do?

What charge was brought against Jason?

What happened to Jason and the brothers?

Where were Paul and Silas hustled off to under cover of darkness?

What did they do here?

Describe the result of Paul and Silas's actions.

Who showed up to cause trouble?

Who was escorted to the coast (about twenty miles away)?
Who stayed in Berea?
Where did Paul go next?

Why was this city so distressing to Paul?
As Paul preached in the synagogue and taught daily in the marketplace, what groups did he encounter?

What meeting did Paul attend?

What "compliment" did Paul have for this group?

Who did Paul make known to them?

Describe the reaction of the crowd.

Where did Paul go next?
Who did Paul meet here?

What trade did Paul practice while staying with this couple?
When was Paul able to devote himself exclusively to preaching?

Why did Paul stop testifying to the Jews in the synagogue?

Who was converted?

Who protected Paul?
How long did Paul preach in this city?

PAUL'S FIRST LETTER TO THE THESSALONIANS
(Corinth, 51 AD)
First Thessalonians

> *As you read this letter, look for Paul's encouragement to stay steadfast even in the face of persecution and for clarification about the second coming of Christ.*

Who wrote this letter?

Who were the recipients?

Who else sent their greetings?

What was commendable about these believers?

How did these men feel about the Thessalonians?

How was Paul "torn away" from them?

Why was the mission team unable to return to see them?

Who was finally able to return? Why was this man sent?

What good news did this man bring back?

What was the Paul's prayer for these Christians?

What exhortations did Paul give them?

Discussion: How do these directives apply today?

What instructions did Paul give about the resurrection?

How will believers know the day when the Lord will return?

What final exhortations did Paul give?

Discussion: How do these directives apply today?

How did Paul end his first letter to the Thessalonians?

PAUL'S SECOND LETTER TO THE THESSALONIANS
(Corinth)
(51–52 AD)
Second Thessalonians; Acts 18:12–22

As you read this letter, look for clarification of Paul's earlier teaching about the second coming of Christ and his emphasis on self-support as the Lord's work is done.

Who wrote this letter?
Who were the recipients of this letter?
What praises did the writer have for these believers?

How would these character traits be rewarded?

What confusion did the writer want to clear up?

What directive did the writer give to these believers?
What prayer request did the writer make?

What warning did the writer give?

Who was proconsul of Achaia (southern Greece)?
Who brought Paul into court?
What was the charge against Paul?

How did the proconsul handle this matter?

How did Paul's accusers respond?

Where did Paul go when he finally left Corinth?

What did Paul do at Cenchrea?
Who stayed at Ephesus?
What was Paul's final destination?

PAUL'S THIRD MISSIONARY JOURNEY
(52/53–55 AD)
Acts 18:23–19:22

> *As you follow Paul on his third missionary journey, look for all the ways he is staying true to his calling.*

(Go to https://theologue.wordpress.com/2014/04/30/zaine-ridling-bible-atlas-e-book/. Use Map 121, "The Third Missionary Journey of Paul," to follow Paul as he carries the gospel message to Galatia, Phyrygia, western Asia, Macedonia, and Achaia.)

Where did Paul go to begin his third missionary journey?

What was Paul doing?

Who was Apollos?

Where did Apollos go to teach people about Jesus?

What did Paul do for some of the disciples when he arrived at Ephesus?

For the first three months, where did Paul go to speak boldly about the kingdom of God?

Why did Paul stop going to this site to teach about Jesus?

What facility did Paul use for the next two years?
In addition to his preaching, how did God use Paul in Ephesus?

Who tried to use Jesus's name to drive out demons?

What happened to these men?

What was the result of this incident?

Where did Paul want to go next?

Who did Paul send to Macedonia?

PAUL'S FIRST LETTER TO THE CORINTHIANS
(Ephesus)
(55 AD)
1 Corinthians; Acts 19:23–20:1

In his letter to the church in Corinth, Paul exhorts the Corinthian Christians to remain steadfast in the face of persecution and to stay faithful to the one true and living God. After reading this section, you should be able to describe some practical life applications of Christian principles.

Who were the recipients of this letter?

How did Paul know about the problems in the Corinthian church?

What issue did Paul first address with this group of believers?

What was Paul's teaching about this problem?

How did Paul say men became righteous, holy, and saved?
How was Paul able to preach so effectively?

How did Paul say believers could understand God's "secret wisdom"?

What kind of mind did Paul say it took to understand God's plan?

What did Paul say was prevented by a worldly mind-set?
What tasks did Paul say were performed by God's servants?

What task did Paul say was performed by God?

Who did Paul say was the foundation of a believer's life?
What will be the test for a life built on this foundation?

What kind of building did Paul use to describe each believer?

Why did Paul rebuke the Corinthians for boasting about who baptized them?

How did Paul say people would be judged?

What warning did Paul give the Corinthians who thought they were better than everyone else because they were Christians?

Describe how Paul thought even the especially chosen apostles were treated.

What appeal did Paul make to the Corinthians?

What specific problem did Paul address next?

What disciplinary action did Paul say should be taken?

What was Paul's teaching about church disputes?

Who did Paul say would *not* inherit the kingdom of God?

What was God's intended purpose for the human body?

In their letter to Paul, what specific concerns did the Corinthian church express?

Discuss the relevance of each of these topics today.

What did Paul say were the advantages of being single over being married?

How long did Paul say a woman was bound to her husband?

What concern did the Corinthians have about eating food sacrificed to idols?

What was Paul's teaching on this subject?

Discussion: We don't participate in animal sacrifice today, but how are Paul's teachings on this subject still applicable?

What freedoms did Paul forfeit so the gospel could be preached?

Why did Paul say he did this?

What analogy did Paul use to describe the value of self-discipline?

Discussion: Why is self-discipline so important in the believer's life?

What lessons could be learned by the example of the Israelites during the exodus?

How did Paul say temptation should be handled?

What did Paul say should drive a Christian's decisions?

What problem was occurring during the Corinthians' meetings?

What was Paul's teaching on the proper way to conduct the Lord's Supper?

What would happen if the Lord's Supper were taken in an unworthy manner?

What did Paul say was the source of spiritual gifts?
Why were these spiritual gifts given?
Make a list of these spiritual gifts.

To what did Paul compare the church?

Make a list of church roles appointed by God.

What did Paul say was the greatest gift?

Describe Paul's teaching about this "greatest gift."

Discussion: How many of these characteristics are found in your "greatest gift"? Are some traits missing? Why?

Why did Paul say the gift of prophecy should be desired more than the gift of speaking in tongues?

Describe the restrictions placed on the use of spiritual gifts.

Who commanded this? Why?

What assurances did Paul give the Corinthians about Christ's resurrection?

What if there was no resurrection?

How did Paul say these believers could be certain of Christ's resurrection?

What did Paul mean by "Bad company corrupts good character"? (1 Corinthians 15:33 quoted from the Greek poet Menander)

Describe the company you keep. How does this teaching apply?

When the Corinthians wanted to know what kind of body they would have at the resurrection, what was Paul's answer?

How was "death swallowed up in victory"? (1 Corinthians 15:54 quoted from Isaiah 25:8)

Discussion: Why is this good news for all believers?

What directives did Paul give about the collection for the church in Jerusalem?

What were Paul's future plans?

Who might be coming to see the Corinthians?

What was included on Paul's short to-do list for the Corinthians?

Discussion: Why is this to-do list still appropriate for believers today?

Who were the first converts in Achaia?

Who had arrived in Ephesus?
What effect did these men have on Paul?
Who sent their greetings to the Corinthians?

Why were Demetrius and the other Ephesian silversmiths so upset about The Way?

What did the silversmiths do?

What did Paul want to do in response?
Why wasn't Paul able to respond in this manner?

Who tried to quiet the crowd?
What success did this man have?

Who finally got the crowd to quiet down? How?

Where did Paul go next?

PAUL'S SECOND LETTER TO THE CORINTHIANS
(Macedonia)
(56–57 AD)
2 Corinthians; Acts 20:2–3

> *As you read this letter, look for teachings from Paul intended to bring this church to spiritual maturity and stability.*

Who were the recipients of this letter?

What lessons did Paul say were learned from suffering?

Describe Paul's travel plans.

When these plans did not work out, what was Paul's defense so as not to appear to have broken his promise to visit?

Who did Paul say provides the strength to stand firm in Christ? How?

Why did Paul write a letter instead of visiting the Corinthians?

How did Paul say troublemakers should be treated?

When Paul went from Ephesus to Troas to preach, who was he hoping to find there?
Where did Paul go next?
Who was leading Paul?

How did Paul compare believers to a smell?

Discussion: What do you "smell" like?

How did Paul compare the believers in Corinth to a letter?

Discussion: What kind of letter are you?

Where did Paul say he gained his competence as a minister?

How did Paul compare the old law to the gospel?

Why was an understanding of the gospel message hidden for some?

How did Paul describe the persecution he experienced?

Why did Paul and the other gospel teachers tolerate this kind of treatment?

What did Paul say was the basis of their faith?

Discussion: What is the basis of a believer's faith today?

How were these gospel teachers able to withstand such persecution?

Discussion: How are believers able to deal with hard times today?

What did Paul say was God's purpose for all people?

Discuss God's purpose for all people today.

Why did Paul say it was important for Christians to please God?

What did Paul say drove him to preach the gospel?

List some of the afflictions Paul endured as a servant of God.

For what was Paul to be commended?

Why should the Corinthians listen to Paul?
What warning did Paul give about relationships with nonbelievers?

Discussion: How does this teaching apply today?

How did Titus's arrival affect Paul?

How did Paul's first letter affect the Corinthians?
How did Paul feel about causing this reaction? Why?

How did the Corinthians react when Titus arrived?

What effect did this reaction have on Titus and Paul?

Describe the example of the Macedonians' generosity.

Why did Paul say all Christians should excel in the grace of giving?

Describe the steps taken to assure the integrity of the collection for the brothers in Judea.

What was Paul's teaching about the correct attitude when giving?

Compare your giving to these directives. Are there areas that could use improvement?

What did Paul say was accomplished by giving?

What was Paul's response to the critics who claimed he lived by the world's standards?

What warning did Paul give about comparisons to the work of others?

Describe Paul as a speaker.

What made Paul such a believable gospel speaker?

What did these sufferings demonstrate about Paul?

Why was Paul "boasting" about his personal experiences?

What final proof did Paul give?

What example did Paul give to show there were others whose spiritual experiences were even more intense than his?

What did Paul say kept him humble?

What ulterior motives had other preachers demonstrated?

What did Paul say was his motive for preaching Christ?
Why was Paul being so defensive?

How many visits would Paul make to Corinth?
What did Paul intend to do on this visit? Why?

What final exhortations did Paul give?

What will be the result if the Corinthians listen to Paul?

When Paul finally made it to Corinth, how long did he remain?

PAUL'S LETTER TO THE ROMANS
(Corinth)
(56/57 AD)
Romans; Acts 20:3–21:16

> *As you read Paul's letter to the Romans, look for evidence of God's faithfulness.*
> *You should be able to explain how righteousness comes through faith in Jesus,*
> *reconciliation comes by God's grace, and respectful obedience is motivated by*
> *an attitude of gratitude.*

How did Paul begin his letter to the Romans?

Where was Paul when he wrote this letter?
Why did Paul say he wanted to visit Rome?

What did Paul say was the theme of the gospel message?

How did Paul say God's eternal power and divine nature were clearly revealed even to the wicked?

How did godless men demonstrate their rejection of God?

What was the result of their rejection?

What did Paul say happened when one man passed judgment on another man's sins?

> *Discussion: How does this lesson about passing judgment apply to all believers?*

Describe God's judgment.

How was righteousness obtained before God?

Why did the Jews think they were spiritually better than the Gentiles?

Explain how these spiritual status markers were insufficient to provide justification before God.

What did Paul say was sufficient to provide justification before God?

What made Abraham the "father of many nations"?

How was Abraham's faith an example for believers?

How are those who have faith able to rejoice in sufferings?

Discussion: How does this teaching apply to believers today?

How did God demonstrate His love for all people, even the ungodly?

Explain how sin entered the world.
What was the consequence of sin?
Who provided a way for this consequence to be overcome?

Explain why God's grace is no excuse for a believer to continue to sin.

What did the law do?

How did Christ provide freedom from the law?

Describe Paul's struggle between the flesh and the spirit.

Why did Paul say sin did not condemn the followers of Christ?

Describe the man who lives by his sinful nature.

Describe the man who lives by the Spirit.

List the benefits of living by the Spirit.

How did Paul describe the role of the Spirit in the lives of believers?

What did Paul say was God's plan for all believers?

What did Paul say could separate believers from God's love?

Describe how this knowledge leads to an attitude of gratitude.

Can the descendants of Abraham be the only children of God's promise? Explain.

What effect did Paul hope the Gentiles' example would have on the Jews?

Why did Paul warn the Gentiles not to get too proud?

Paul did not want the Romans to be ignorant about a mystery. What was this mystery?

In light of God's mercy, how did Paul say believers should live?

How did Paul compare those in Christ to a human body?

Make a list of the godly gifts mentioned by Paul.

Discussion: How has God gifted you?

How did Paul say these gifts were to be used?

What kinds of deeds should believers do?

How did Paul say God's people should treat others?

Discussion: Why is it sometimes difficult to treat people this way?

What did Paul say the Christian's duty should be toward governing authorities?

Discussion: Why is it sometimes difficult to have this attitude toward those in power?

How did Paul say Christians should respond in disputable matters?

How should the stronger Christian treat the weaker one?

What did Paul say was the purpose of his letter to the Romans?

Describe Paul's future travel plans.

What was Paul's prayer request?

Who was Phoebe?

To whom did Paul send special greetings?

What warning did Paul give about potential troublemakers?

Who sent greetings from Corinth to Rome?

How did Paul end his letter to the Romans?

(Troas, Miletus, Tyre, Caesarea, and Jerusalem)
(Spring)
(58 AD)
Acts 20:3–21:16

What delayed Paul's voyage to Syria and Jerusalem?

Who sailed on ahead to Troas?

Where did Paul go?
When did he leave this city?
Where did Paul go next?

How long did the group stay here?
Why did Paul and the believers get together on the first day of the week?

How long did Paul speak?
What happened as Paul talked on and on?

How did Paul respond to this accident?

(Go to https://theologue.wordpress.com/2014/04/30/zaine-ridling-bible-atlas-e-book/. Use
Map 121 again to trace Paul's journey from Assos to Miletus.)

How did the group get to Assos?
How did Paul get to Assos?
How did the group get to Miletus?

Why did Paul decide to sail past Ephesus?

Who did Paul ask to come to Miletus?
What did Paul tell these men about his mission?

What warnings did Paul give to these men?

Describe Paul's parting from these men.

(Go to https://theologue.wordpress.com/2014/04/30/zaine-ridling-bible-atlas-e-book/. Look at Map 121 again. Trace Paul's journey from Miletus to Caesarea.)

Trace Paul's journey from Miletus to Caesarea.

Where did Paul and his group stay in Caesarea?

Who was Agabus?
What was Agabus's message for Paul?

Describe the crowd's reaction to this news.

Where did Paul and his group stay in Jerusalem?

PAUL'S ARREST AND TRIAL
BEFORE THE SANHEDRIN
(Jerusalem at Pentecost and Caesarea)
(58 AD?)
Acts 21:17–23:35

How did his Christian brothers receive Paul when he arrived in Jerusalem?
Why did Paul go see James and the Jerusalem elders?

What problem did these men have with Paul's teachings?

What did the elders ask Paul to do?

How did Paul respond to this request?

What happened to Paul while he was at the temple?

Who came to Paul's rescue?

What request did Paul make?
What language did Paul use?
How did Paul describe himself?

How did the Jewish crowd respond when Paul stated his mission?

What order did the Roman commander give?

What caused the Roman commander to change his order?

What happened the next day?

What was Paul's defense before this group?

Why did Paul use this defense?

What happened as a result of Paul's statement?

On the following night, who appeared to Paul?
What was the message?

Who formed a conspiracy to kill Paul?

Who warned Paul about this conspiracy?

How did the commander respond when given this information?

What happened to Paul when he reached Caesarea?

PAUL BEFORE GOVERNOR FELIX, GOVERNOR FESTUS, AND KING AGRIPPA
(Caesarea)
(58–60 AD)
Acts 24:1–26:32

How long did it take for Paul's accusers to arrive in Caesarea?
Who came to accuse Paul?
How did the lawyer begin his case against Paul?

What charges did the lawyer bring against Paul?

Recount Paul's defense.

What did Governor Felix decide to do with Paul?

Why did Governor Felix send for Paul several days later?

Why did Governor Felix frequently visit with Paul?
How long was Paul detained?
What happened to Governor Felix at the end of this time?
Who became the new governor?
Why did the Jews want Paul's trial moved to Jerusalem?

What was the outcome of Paul's trial before this new governor?

How did Festus handle this situation?

Describe Paul's response to this request.

Who arrived in Caesarea a few days later?
Why did Paul say he was fortunate to have an audience with this man?

Recount Paul's defense before King Agrippa.

How did Governor Festus respond?

How did this king respond?

PAUL'S VOYAGE TO ROME
(Caesarea, Crete, Malta, and Rome)
(60 AD)
Acts 27:1–28:15

(Go to https://theologue.wordpress.com/2014/04/30/zaine-ridling-bible-atlas-e-book/. Use Map 123, "Paul's Voyage to Rome," to trace Paul's journey from Caesarea to Rome.)

Who took charge of Paul?

Who else was on this voyage?

Trace Paul's travels from Caesarea to Crete.

Why was the voyage so dangerous?

What was Paul's warning?

What did Julius the centurion decide to do?

What happened when the group set sail?

What was Paul's message during this difficult time?

After two weeks of being driven by the storm, what did the sailors attempt to do?

What was Paul's warning?
How did the soldiers respond to Paul's warning?

Describe what happened just before dawn.

Describe what happened at daylight.

How did the soldiers respond? Why?

How did Julius the centurion respond?

Where was the group shipwrecked?
How did the islanders receive the group?

What happened to Paul as he helped gather wood for the fire?

How did Paul react?

Describe the islanders' reaction.

Who was the chief official on this island?

How did this man treat the castaways?

Who did Paul heal?

How long did Paul and his group stay on this island?
How was the group finally able to get to Rome?

PAUL UNDER HOUSE ARREST IN ROME
(Rome)
(61–63 AD)
Acts 28:16–31

What happened to Paul when he reached Rome?

Who did Paul invite to come to his home? Why?

How did these men respond to Paul?

How did the people respond to Paul's preaching about Jesus?

How long did Paul preach under these circumstances in Rome?

PAUL'S LETTER TO THE COLOSSIANS
(Roman Prison)
(61–63 AD)
The Letter to the Colossians

> *After reading this letter, you should be able to explain how faith, hope, and love transform believers into Christ. You should also be able to explain how the supremacy of Christ and the fullness of the gospel message can be used to solve all church issues.*

(Go to https://theologue.wordpress.com/2014/04/30/zaine-ridling-bible-atlas-e-book/. Look at Map 123 again. Use this map to locate Colossae, Laodicea, and Hierapolis.)

Where was Paul when he wrote this letter?

Who was with Paul?

Who was Epaphras?

Why was Paul thankful for the brothers in Christ at Colossae?

What was Paul's prayer for the Colossians?

How did Paul say these qualities would benefit their spiritual lives?

How did Paul describe Christ?

What did Christ's death do for the Colossians and for all believers?

What did Paul say was the "mystery kept hidden for ages"?

What did Paul way were the "glorious riches" of this mystery?

Why was Paul concerned about this group of Christians?

What was the sign of the old covenant with God?

What did Paul say was the sign of the new covenant with God?

How did Paul say believers were made "alive in Christ"?

What did Paul say should be the focus of a believer's life?
What was causing the Colossians to risk being disqualified from the prize of a home in heaven?
Where did Paul say the hearts and minds of Christians should be set?

How did Paul say Christians' lives should be transformed?

Discussion: At what stage is your transformation? How would you describe your relationship with Christ?

How did Paul say God's chosen people should "put on Christ"?

What did Paul say should rule the heart of a Christian?
According to Paul, how should Christians behave?

Discussion: How would you rate your Christlike behavior?

How did Paul say Christ was to be reflected in the following relationships?
Marriage

Family

Master/Slave

Individual
Outsiders

Who was Tychicus?

Who was Onesimus?

Who else was with Paul in Rome?

What was to be done with Paul's letter to the Colossians?

PAUL'S LETTER TO PHILEMON
(Roman Prison)
(61–63 AD)
Letter to Philemon

> *After reading this letter, you should be able to explain why it was written. You should also be able to compare Paul's intercession for Onesimus to Christ's intercession for us.*

Where was Paul when he wrote this letter?
To whom did Paul write this personal letter?

Why did Paul say he thanked God for Philemon?

On what basis was Paul making his appeal?
For whom did Paul make his appeal?

Why did Paul say it might have been necessary for this slave to be separated from his master?

What favor did Paul ask of Philemon?

What did Paul offer to do?
Of what did Paul remind Philemon?
What did Paul say he thought Philemon would do about this situation?

Who else sent their greetings?

PAUL'S LETTER TO THE EPHESIANS
(Roman Prison)
(61–63 AD)
Letter to the Ephesians

> *After reading this letter, you should be able to explain God's plan of salvation and describe the relationship between Christ and His church. You should also be able to provide examples of the practical application of this knowledge in the lives of believers and explain why unity is so important.*

Who were the recipients of this letter written by Paul?

When did Paul say God set His plan of salvation in motion?

Why did Paul say God wanted to "adopt" believers as His sons?

What role did Jesus Christ play in God's plan of salvation?

What did Paul say sealed the believer's hope in Christ?

What was Paul's prayer for the Ephesians?

How did God demonstrate His great power?

Describe the Ephesians' previous spiritual status.

How did God deal with their sinful status? Why?

> *Discussion: Compare the status of the ancient Ephesians to that of people today. What is the present-day solution for this status problem?*

What did Paul say was the key element in God's plan of salvation?

What did Paul say could not provide righteousness?

Why did Paul say God created man?

> *Discussion: Why were you created?*

Describe the Gentiles' previous spiritual status.

Describe the Gentiles' current spiritual status.

How did Paul say Jesus broke down the barrier between the Jews and the Gentiles?

How did Paul describe these non-Jewish Christians?

How did Paul say this household was constructed?

What mystery did Paul reveal?

How did Paul say God's wisdom has been made known?

What was Paul's prayer for the Ephesians?

What exhortation did Paul have for the church at Ephesus?

> *Discussion: What practical application do these traits have for your life?*

List the "ones."

What gifts did Paul say Christ gave to the church? Why?

> *Discussion: What do you see as your gift(s)?*

What did Paul say was the danger of "infant" knowledge?

> *Discussion: Where are you in the development of your knowledge? Infancy? Childhood? Adolescence? Young Adulthood? Adulthood? Mature Christian?*

How did Paul say this danger could be avoided?

What personal exhortations did Paul have for the Ephesians?

Discussion: How do you deal with anger? How would you describe your "talk"? How would you describe your ability to forgive?

Who did Paul say the Ephesian believers should imitate?

Who will *not* inherit the kingdom of Christ and of God?

How did Paul say Christians should live?

Discussion: How is your light shining?

What exhortation did Paul give about interpersonal relationships?
Husband/Wife?

Parent/Child?

Master/Servant?

God/Christian?

What did Paul say was needed to stand against the devil's schemes? Describe this equipment.

Describe the condition of your armor.

What kind of struggle did Paul say was taking place?

Who did Paul say was the opponent in this struggle?

Who carried this letter to Ephesus?

How did Paul end this letter?

PAUL'S LETTER TO THE PHILIPPIANS
(Roman Prison)
(61–63 AD)
Letter to the Philippians

> *After you read this letter, you should be able to describe the heartfelt emotions and core character traits necessary to build and maintain strong Christlike relationships.*

Where was Paul when he wrote this letter?
To whom did Paul write this letter?

How did Paul feel about this group of believers?

What was Paul's prayer for the Philippians?

Why did Paul say his imprisonment was a blessing?

According to Paul, what motivated some to preach about Christ?

Why did Paul say he preached the gospel?

Explain Paul's dilemma.

What exhortation did Paul give the Philippians about unity?

What exhortation did Paul give about humility?

Discussion: In a fair self-evaluation, how would you rate your level of humility?

What exhortation did Paul give the Philippians about effort?

Discussion: In an honest self-evaluation, how would you rate your level of effort? Complaining? Arguing? Sacrifice?

How did Paul describe the example set by children of God in a crooked and depraved world?

How brightly shining is your starlight?

Who was Paul sending to Philippi?

Why was Paul sending these two men?

What warning did Paul have for the Philippians?

How did Paul describe his Jewish heritage?

What did Paul trade for confidence in his heritage and in the old law's ability to bring salvation?

Discussion: How do believers exchange self-confidence for confidence in Christ?

What did Paul say was his goal in life?

Discussion: What are your goals in life?

How did Paul describe the "enemies of the cross of Christ"?

How did Paul describe citizens of heaven?

Name the two Philippian Christian sisters who were having a dispute.

What advice did Paul give to these two women?

How did Paul say this situation could be reconciled?

What kind of thinking did Paul say would bring God's peace?

> *Discussion: How many of these attributes apply to your thought processes?*

How was Paul able to feel contentment given his situation?

How had the Philippians supported Paul?

PAUL'S FIRST LETTER TO TIMOTHY
(63–64 AD)
1 Timothy

> *As you read this letter, look for Paul's instructions to a young preacher on false doctrine, faith building, church organization, powerful prayer, and effective ministry. You should also be able to explain the role of women, list the qualifications for elders and deacons, and give spiritual advice on how to treat fellow Christians.*

Where was Paul when he wrote this letter?
Who was the recipient of this personal, pastoral letter?
Where was this man?

What problem was this man apparently facing?

How was Paul's life an example in this situation?

Why did Paul give instruction to this young evangelist?

Why had Paul given up on Hymenaeus and Alexander?

Why did Paul urge Christians to pray for everyone, even those in authority?

What did Paul say God wanted for all men?

How did Paul say women should dress for worship?

What did Paul say was the woman's role in worship?

List the qualifications for an elder or overseer of the church.

List the qualifications for a church deacon.

What was Paul's reason for sending these instructions?

What did Paul say was the answer to the "mystery of godliness"?

What negative influences did Paul say would cause some to walk away from their faith?

What specific ministerial instructions did Paul have for this young evangelist?

What did Paul say was this young man's gift?

What advice did Paul give this young preacher about how to treat others?

How did Paul say widows were to be treated?

How did Paul say elders/overseers were to be treated?

How did Paul say slaves were to treat their masters?

Discussion: How can Paul's personal relationship advice be applied to your life?

What characteristics did Paul say could be found in false teachers?

What did Paul say the Christian's attitude should be toward riches?

What did Paul say should be pursued instead of riches?

How did Paul say earthly wealth was to be used?

What was Paul's final warning?

PAUL'S LETTER TO TITUS
(63–65 AD)
Letter to Titus

> *Make a list of the instructions for young evangelists provided by Paul to both Timothy and Titus.*

Where was Paul when he wrote this letter?

Where was Titus? Why?

List the qualifications for being an elder.

What specific problem did Paul address?

How did Paul say Titus should fight this problem?
What should be taught to older men?

What should Titus teach to older women?

What should Titus teach to younger men?

What should Titus teach to slaves?

What did Paul say was the basis for these teachings?

How did Paul say this knowledge should change the lives of believers?

Why did Paul say grace demanded believers live a changed life?

Discussion: As a believer, how has your life changed?

Describe how Paul felt about religious quarrels.

Who was Paul trying to send to Crete? Why?

Who carried this letter to Titus?

PAUL'S SECOND LETTER TO TIMOTHY
(64–67 AD)
2 Timothy

> *As you read Paul's final letter, look for evidence of his loneliness and suffering as he faces the end of his life. Also, look for his encouragement to stay strong in the face of opposition and always be prepared to defend the faith.*

Where does it appear Paul was when he wrote this second letter to Timothy?

Describe Paul's relationship with Timothy.

What kind of spirit would be needed to get through the coming trials?

What did Paul encourage Timothy to do with his gift of ministry?

How did Paul describe his own ministry?

What did Paul tell Timothy to keep preaching?

How was religious persecution affecting some believers?

Who stayed faithful?

Describe the three analogies Paul used to encourage Timothy in his ministry.

Discussion: Which of these analogies best describes your faith walk?

Who was Paul thinking about while he was in prison?

Explain how a believer "dies to live."

What instruction did Paul give Timothy about his teaching?

What prediction did Paul make about the future?

How did Paul say his life was an example for Timothy?

Discussion: How was Paul's life an example for all believers?

Describe the purpose of all Scripture.

What charge did Paul give to Timothy?

What was about to happen to Paul?
Describe Paul's attitude toward this situation.

Discussion: What does it take to be able to face death with an attitude like Paul's?

What did Paul ask Timothy to do?

Describe the trouble caused by Alexander.

Who was at Paul's side during his first defense?

Who did Paul say would rescue him?

Who did Paul ask to be greeted at the church in Ephesus?

Additional Letters Written to Spread the Gospel Message

(50–95 AD)

JAMES'S LETTER
(50–60 AD?)
James

> *As you read this letter, look for characteristics of genuine faith and genuine wisdom. You should also be able to explain the correlation between good deeds and faith.*

Which James was most likely the author of this letter?

Who were the recipients?

What was happening to Christians during this time?
How did James say believers should handle trials? Why?

Discussion: How do you handle trials?

What did James say believers should do when uncertain?

Discussion: How do you handle uncertainty?

Why should a believer's confidence *not* be placed in earthly possessions?

Why did James say a man who persevered was blessed?

What did James say was the source of temptation?

Discussion: How do you respond when tempted?

How did James say a believer should handle anger?

Discussion: How do you handle anger?

Why did James say knowledge of the Word was not enough?

What did James say was at the core of true religion?

What act of judgment did James prohibit for Christians?
What is the penalty for this sin?

What did James say should be seen in the life of a believer as evidence of faith?

Discussion: Do your good deeds demonstrate a genuine faith? Why or why not?

What did James have to say about those who teach the gospel?

What analogies did James use to describe the power of the tongue?

Discussion: Do you have power over your tongue or does your tongue have power over you?

How did James say a wise, understanding person could be recognized?

Describe earthly wisdom.

Describe heavenly wisdom.

Discussion: Which of these types of wisdom best describe you?

What did James say happened when people became materialistic?

How did James say godliness was achieved?

Why did James say no one should speak against a brother?

How did James say worldly people plan for tomorrow?

How did James say God's people should plan for tomorrow?

Discussion: How do you plan for tomorrow?

What did James say would happen to those who oppressed the saints?

What did James say should be the attitude of believers during times of oppression and suffering?

Discussion: What is your attitude during times of suffering?

How did James say a believer's verbal agreement should be guaranteed?

What should all believers do in the midst of suffering?

What kind of prayers did James say will be answered?

Why did James say sins should be confessed?

Discussion: How do you feel after you confess a wrong?

How did James say believers should treat a brother who wanders away from God?

JUDE'S LETTER
(60–80 AD?)
Jude

> As you read this letter, look for instructions on how to handle false teachers
> and for a caution about keeping the faith.

How did the author identify himself?

What did the author want to write about?

What was the subject of this letter instead?

What were these godless men teaching?

What historical examples were used as a comparison to these false teachers?

What were these "dreamers" doing?

What did Jude say was going to happen to these ungodly men?

What caution did Jude give to the faithful?

Discussion: What application does this caution have for all believers?
In his benediction, what did Jude write in praise to God?

PETER'S FIRST LETTER
(60–64 AD?)
1 Peter

> *As you read this letter, look for statements that give hope in the face of suffering and exhort all believers to remain steadfast and sure during difficult times. You should be able to describe the life application of Christian principles motivated by an understanding of how precious God's children are to Him.*

(Go to https://theologue.wordpress.com/2014/04/30/zaine-ridling-bible-atlas-e-book/. Use Map 128, "The Roman Empire in the Early Second Century," to get an idea about the geographic area under Roman rule at this time.)

Review what is known about Peter.

Who were the recipients of this letter from Peter?

How did Peter describe these Christians?

Describe how each entity of the Trinity is involved in the plan of salvation.

Why did Peter say God was to be praised?

Discussion: What does the phrase "living hope" mean to you?

What did Peter say would have to be faced before salvation came?

What did Peter say were the benefits of trials?

Discussion: Describe a time of trial in your life. How did suffering refine your faith?

How did Peter define faith?

How did Peter say believers should respond in light of God's grace?

Who did Peter say had redeemed all people?

How did Peter say believers became "born again"?

List some characteristics of the old creature.

>   *Discussion: How many "old creature" characteristics do you still have?*

List some characteristics of the new creature.

>   *Discussion: How many "new creature" characteristics do you have?*

How did Peter compare believers to "living stones"?

Why did Peter describe followers of Christ as a "holy priesthood"?

How did Peter say Christians should conduct themselves?

>   *Discussion: Why is it so important for believers to live transformed lives?*

How did Peter say Christians should behave toward those in authority?

How did Peter say Christian slaves should behave toward their masters?

Who did Peter say was the believer's example when it came to unjust treatment?

How did Peter say Christian wives should behave toward their husbands?

How did Peter say Christian husbands should treat their wives?

How did Peter say all Christians should behave toward each other?

Discussion: Why is it so important for Christians to demonstrate this type of behavior?

How did Peter say Christians could have confidence during difficult times?

What did Peter say was the result of Christ's death?

What did Peter say was the significance of the floodwaters during Noah's days?

What did Peter say this water symbolized now?

Why did Peter say the gospel was preached?

What attributes did Peter say should be found in those who live according to God?

Discussion: How are these Christian principles being applied in your life?

What did Peter say a Christian's attitude should be toward suffering?

Describe the special message Peter gave to the elders.

What character trait did Peter say should be found in all Christians?

Who did Peter say was the enemy?
How did Peter describe this enemy?

How did Peter say this enemy could be resisted?

Who helped write this letter?
Who else was with Peter at this time?

PETER'S SECOND LETTER
(64 AD)
2 Peter

As you read this second letter, look for Peter's advice on how to handle false teachers and how believers can protect themselves from false teaching. You should also be able to describe what will happen on judgment day.

Who were the recipients of this second letter from Peter?
What did Peter say God has given to those who know Him?

What qualities did Peter say believers should add to their faith? Why?

Why was it so important for Peter to remind his fellow Christians of these things at this time?

What made Peter such a credible source of information about Jesus?

What did Peter say was another credible source of information about Jesus?

What warning did Peter give?

What evidence did Peter give to prove the wicked will be punished by God?

What examples did Peter give to demonstrate the righteous will be rescued by God?

How did Peter describe these false teachers?

How did Peter describe the results of their false teaching?

Why did Peter write his letters to Christians?

Who did Peter say will come in "the last days"?

Why did Peter say God has delayed the second coming of the Lord?

Discussion: What is "time" to God?

When did Peter say the Lord will come again?

According to Peter, what effect should the prospect of judgment day have on the lives of Christians?

Discussion: What effect does the prospect of judgment day have on your life?

Whose writings did Peter mention as being in agreement with his?
What was Peter's final warning?

How did Peter say this potential fall could be avoided?

THE LETTER TO THE HEBREWS

(65–70 AD?)

Letter to the Hebrews

> As you read this letter, look for exhortations to hold tightly to the faith and faithfully follow the new covenant. Also look for warnings about ignoring the message, falling away, rejecting the Savior, and engaging in thankless worship to God. After reading this letter, you should be able to present an effective defense of the Christian faith.

Who wrote this letter?

To whom was this letter written?

What is known about the author?

According to the writer, how did God speak to the Hebrews in the past?

How does God speak to people today?

According to the writer, which is superior—the old law or Christ's message?

According to the writer, who is superior—Christ or the angels?

What will happen if Christ's salvation message is rejected?

What confirmed the Lord's salvation message?

How did Christ's change in status demonstrate God's grace?

How did Christ's act of becoming a man give hope to all people?

According to the writer, who is superior—Moses or Christ?

Describe the sin of unbelief.

What happened to the Israelites when they lost faith in God?

According to the writer, who is superior—Joshua or Christ?

> *Discussion: Why do you think the writer wanted to establish Christ's superiority over the old law, angels, Moses, and Joshua?*

What will God's obedient, faithful believers receive?

What will prevent some from receiving this promise?
How did the writer describe the Word of God?

How did the writer compare Jesus to a high priest?

Why did the writer say this concept was so hard to understand?

Make a list of elementary Christian teachings.

What happens when those who believe in God fall away?

Describe the analogy used to make the point about the danger of falling away.

In this analogy, what does the rain represent? The land? The crop? The thorns and thistles? The worthless land?

Why did the writer say he could have confidence in the Hebrews' faith?

Describe the example given by the writer of diligent, patient faithfulness.

According to the writer, what two things never change with God?

Who was Melchizedek?

What was the role of a high priest like Aaron and other priests from the tribe of Levi?

How was Christ a priest in the same way as Melchizedek?

How did Christ represent a change in the priesthood?

When the priesthood changed, what else had to change?

Who became the guarantee of a better covenant?
How is this new covenant greater than the old one?

According to the first covenant, what was in the earthly tabernacle's first room, or Holy Place?

What was behind the curtain in the second room, or Most Holy Place?

What was in the ark of the covenant?

Under the old law, who was the only person allowed to enter the Most Holy Place and be in the presence of God?
How often did he enter this area of the tabernacle?
Why did he enter?

Under the new covenant, who symbolically entered the Most Holy Place?

How often did He enter?
Why did He enter?

What has to happen before a will (covenant) can become valid?

What validated the old covenant?

What validated the new covenant?

What did the writer say man was destined to do?

What will happen when Christ appears a second time?

According to the writer, what did Christ's sacrifice replace?

What was established instead?

Under the new covenant, how are all believers able to be in the presence of God?

What did the writer say was the proper response to this new open access to God?

How did the writer say believers should motivate one another?

What did the writer say would be the consequences of willful sin?

During the early days of their Christianity, how did the Hebrews respond to persecution?

Why did the writer say faithful perseverance was so important?

How did the writer define faith?

> *Give an example of faith in something that cannot be seen. Discuss some other examples of being sure of unseen things.*

List some early patriarchs who were examples of great faith.

List some judges, kings, and prophets who also had great faith.

List some actions of great faith.

Give some examples of how God's faithful followers were persecuted.

How should these examples influence the lives of all believers?

Discussion: How have these examples of great faith influenced your life?

How did the writer say the believer's race of faith was to be run?

Discussion: How are you doing in your faith race?

How should Christ's example of perseverance encourage believers?

How did the writer say believers should view their struggles?

Discussion: How do you view your earthly struggles?

Why did the writer say believers should live holy lives?

Describe God's judgment under the old law.
Describe God's judgment under the new covenant.

For what did Abel's spilled blood cry out?
For what does Christ's spilled blood cry out?
How did the writer describe proper worship before God?
What did the writer say could not be removed or shaken?
What general advice did the writer give the Hebrews on how to strengthen their faith?

Discussion: How does this advice apply to believers today?

How did the writer describe the teachings of Jesus?

What kind of teachings should be avoided?

Under the old covenant, how was sin removed?

Under the new covenant, how is sin removed?

Under the new covenant, what sacrifices are pleasing to God?

According to the writer, how are church leaders to be treated?

What prayers did the writer request?
What prayers were given for the recipients of this letter?

Who did the writer say had just been released from prison?
Where might the writer have been when he wrote this letter?

JOHN'S FIRST LETTER
(90–95 AD)
1 John

> *As you read John's first letter, look for his encouragement to walk in the light and his warning to watch out for antichrists. After reading this letter, you should be able to describe a true believer and to explain the assurances all believers have in Christ.*

Who was John?

Where might John have been when he wrote this letter?

Who were the recipients of this letter?

How did John describe Jesus?

Why was John such a credible source of information about Jesus?

Why did John testify about Jesus?

How did John describe God?
How did John describe those who say they are in a relationship with God but do not live their faith?

How did John describe those who live their faith as true believers?

According to John, who sins?

According to John, how does God respond to confessed sins?

What role did John say Jesus Christ plays when sins are confessed?

How did John describe those who say they know God but do not obey His commands?

How does God feel about those who obey His commands?

What did John say was the true test of a life lived in the light?

Describe your walk in the light.

Who are those who walk in the light called to love? What are they told *not* to love?

What warning did John give about false teachers?

What truth do these false teachers deny?
According to John, how can believers know the truth?

What reward is promised for believers who hold on to the truth?
How did John describe those who follow the Word?

How did John say those who follow the Word deal with sin?

How are children of God recognizable?

How are children of the devil recognizable?
According to John, how did Jesus Christ demonstrate true love for the world?

How did John say God's children demonstrate love?

According to John, what does obedience bring?

List the two most fundamental commands for God's children.
According to John, what lives in all believers?

List six ways nonbelievers can be distinguished from believers.

According to John, what three things testify about Jesus?

What assurances did John give to believers?

According to John, who keeps believers safe from sin?
According to John, who has control of all sinful, worldly things like idolatry?

JOHN'S SECOND LETTER
(90–95 AD)
2 John

> *As you read this personal letter from John, look for repeated messages from his first letter.*

Who was the recipient of this personal letter from John?

What important messages are repeated from John's first letter?

Why was this letter kept short?

JOHN'S THIRD LETTER
(90–95 AD)
3 John

Who was the recipient of this personal letter from John?

Why was John joyful?

How was this person's faithfulness being demonstrated?

Who was causing problems in the church? What was this man doing?

Who did John commend? Why?

Why was this letter kept short?

The End of the Journey

(95–96 AD)

> *Everything you have read up to this point has helped prepare you for the final stage of your chronological journey through the Bible. God's plan of redemption provides encouragement for and enlightenment about what the future holds for all believers. After reading Revelation, you should be able to describe John's vision and prophecy pertaining to Christ's ultimate battle with Satan and His decisive defeat of evil. There is absolute victory in Jesus!*

THE REVELATION TO JOHN
Revelation

Use the map of the "Seven Churches of Revelation" to locate the towns mentioned by John.

Who was the emperor of Rome at this time?
Who revealed this prophecy to John?
Identify the central theme of this revelation.

What was the purpose of this revelation?

Who sends their salutations?

What praises were given to God and Christ?

Where was John when he received this revelation?

What day of the week was it?
How did this revelation come to John?

List the seven churches of Asia.

When John turned to identify who was speaking, what did he see?

Describe John's reaction to this vision.

How do you imagine you might react to such a vision?

What did the vision say to John?

What do the seven stars represent?
What do the seven lampstands represent?

COMPARISON OF THE LETTERS TO THE SEVEN CHURCHES OF ASIA

	Ephesus	Smyrna	Pergamum	Thyatira	Sardis	Philadelphia	Laodicea
	Capital city, chief commercial port, site of temple to Diana, 24,000 seat theatre, Paul evangelized this city on 2nd and 3rd missionary journeys, Timothy preached here	Beautiful, prosperous export city, site of many pagan temples including a Temple to the Emperor, was a stronghold for Imperial Cult worship	Situated on cone shaped hill 1,000 ft. above Caicus Valley, ancient library w/ 200,000 volumes, site of 1st temple to Caesar and temple to Zeus, Roman political center	Military outpost, home of bronze metal workers and garment dying, famous for purple colored cloth called "turkey red"	Natural citadel 1,500 ft up on top of Mt. Tmolus, wealthy city, site of temple to Diana, city full of paganism, stong Jewish community	"The Gateway to the East", an important commercial city on well traveled trade route, center of wine production and worship to Dionysus, god of wine and fertility, located on a fault line	Wealthiest city in Phrygia, known for banking & textile industries, site of a medical school and production of famous eye salve (collyrium), known for soft, glossy black wool used in carpets and cloaks, hot water piped in from hot springs in nearby Hieropolis
Praises							

Problems							
Potential Risk							
Promised Reward							

Fill in the comparison chart of the letters to the seven churches. List praises, problems, potential risk, and promised reward.

What did John see next?
What did John hear?

Through the Spirit, what was John able to see?

What was in the center of these thrones?
Describe (or draw) each creature.

What were the twenty-four elders doing?

What was in the right hand of the One on the throne?

Why did John cry and cry?

What made John stop crying?

What did John see next?

What did this creature do?

How was this creature able to open the scroll?

What did John hear next?

SEVEN SEALS

Seal	Rider	Horse	Object	Purpose
First				
Second				
Third				
Fourth				
Fifth				
Sixth				
Seventh				

Fill in the chart of the seven seals.

After the sixth seal was opened, who did John see?

What were these angels doing?

Who called out to these angels? What was the message?

Who was sealed?
Who did John see next?

Who were the ones in white robes?

Discussion: Do you see yourself in this crowd dressed in a white robe? Why or why not?

After the seventh seal was opened, what did the seven angels prepare to do?

SEVEN ANGELS AND SEVEN TRUMPETS

First Angel & First Trumpet	
Second Angel & Second Trumpet	
Third Angel & Third Trumpet	
Fourth Angel & Fourth Trumpet	
Fifth Angel & Fifth Trumpet	
Sixth Angel & Sixth Trumpet	
Seventh Angel & Seventh Trumpet	

Fill in the chart of the seven angels and seven trumpets. Describe what happened when the first four trumpets were sounded.

Describe (or draw) the creatures released when the fifth trumpet sounded.

What were these creatures told to do?

Identify the first woe.

Who was the king over these creatures?

Describe (or draw) the mounted troops released when the sixth trumpet sounded.

What effect did this destruction have on the survivors?

What did John see before the seventh trumpet sounded?

What did this vision do?

What was John told to do with the object in this angel's hand?

What would be the result?

What was John given next?
What was John told to do with this object?

What were the two witnesses empowered to do?

What was to happen when the witnesses' testimony was completed?

What happened after the seventh trumpet sounded?

What great and wondrous signs appeared in heaven?

What war took place in heaven?

What was the outcome?

Who did the dragon pursue?
How did the dragon try to attack this individual?

Out of frustration, who did the dragon go after next?

What came up out of the sea?

Describe (or draw) this creature.

What power was given to this creature?

How did this beast use this power?

What creature came out of the earth?

What power did this creature exercise?

What mark was placed on this creature's followers? Why?

Who did John see next?

What did John hear?

When John looked up, what did he see?

Discussion: How do these angels' messages apply to people today?

What exhortation did John have for the saints?

Discussion: How does this exhortation apply to believers today?

Who did John see seated on a white cloud?

What did the temple angel tell this vision to do?
Who else came out of the temple?

What did this second angel do? What was the result of this angel's actions?

When John looked up into heaven, what did he see?

Who did John see standing by a fiery sea of glass?

When the temple opened, who came out?

What did one of the four living creatures give to these visions?

SEVEN ANGELS AND SEVEN BOWLS]

Bowl	Poured out on	Result
First		
Second		
Third		
Fourth		
Fifth		
Sixth		
Seventh		

Fill in the chart of the seven angels and the seven bowls.

What did John see after the sixth angel poured out his bowl?

Describe (or draw) the "great prostitute."

Discuss your reaction to the description of this woman.

What explanation did the angel give to John about this scene?

What did the angel say the seven heads represented?

Who did the angel say was the eighth king?

What did the angel say the ten horns represented?

Who will win the war between the beast and the Lamb?

What did the angel say was represented by the waters on which the "great prostitute" sits?

What did the angel say the woman represented?

Who did John see next?

What was this vision's message?

What warning was given by a voice from heaven?

Discussion: How does this warning apply to people today?

How will the kings of the earth react when they see Babylon's punishment?

How will the merchants of the earth react when they see Babylon in ruins?

How will the sea captains, sailors, and sea merchants react when they see Babylon burning?

What object did a mighty angel use to demonstrate Babylon's destruction?

What did John hear next?

Discussion: How do you imagine you might feel if you heard this celebration?

In John's vision, what wedding was about to take place?

Describe (or draw) the horse and rider in John's vision.

Discussion: How do you imagine you might react to this vision?

Who followed this horse and rider?

What was coming out of the mouth of this rider?

What name was written on His robe and thigh?
What did an angel tell the birds to do?

What happened to the beast and the false prophet?

What happened to the kings of the earth and their armies?

What did the angel from heaven have in his possession?

What did this angel do with these items?

Who else did John see in heaven?

According to John's Revelation, what will happen to Satan when the thousand years are over?

Describe what John saw next.

Who did John see standing before this vision?

What was taking place?
From where did the dead come?
What happened to those whose names were *not* written in the Book of Life?

What is the second death?
After this great judgment, what did John see?

What city did John see?

What did the loud voice coming from the throne tell John?

Discussion: What feelings and emotions are inspired by the vision of this "new Jerusalem"?

How did God describe Himself to John?

What did God say would happen to the cowardly, unbelieving, vile, murderers, sexually immoral, those who practice magic arts, the idolaters, and all liars?

What did one of the seven angels who had the seven bowls show John?

Describe (or draw) this holy city.

What structure was obviously missing from this great holy city? Why?

What security measure was unnecessary in this great holy city?

What and who will never be allowed to enter this holy city?

Who will be allowed to enter this holy city?

Discussion: What application does this message have for people today?

What river did the angel show John?
Describe (or draw) this river.

What did John see on each side of the river?

Who will serve God and the Lamb in this kingdom city?

How long will this kingdom reign?

How has the truth of this revelation been verified?

How did Jesus describe Himself?

Who has been invited to enjoy the blessings offered by the Spirit and the bride?

What caution did John give?

Discussion: How does this warning apply today?

Who promised to come soon?
How did John respond to this promise?

Discussion: What is your response to this promise?

How did John end this writing?

Academic Year Study Schedule (36 weeks)

Week 1	In the Beginning	pgs. 1-10
Week 2	Jacob and Esau	pgs. 11-22
Week 3	Covenant Established between God and Israel	pgs. 23-32
Week 4	Joshua, Israel's New Leader	pgs. 32-41
Week 5	The Israelites' Arrival in Canaan: The Beginning of Life in the Promised Land	pgs. 42-53
Week 6	Samson	pgs. 54-62
Week 7	David and His Psalms	pgs. 62-75
Week 8	Psalms For a Troubled Soul	pgs. 75-77
Week 9	King Solomon	pgs. 77-82
Week 10	Solomon's Proverbs, Song of Songs, & Ecclesiastes	pgs. 83-95
Week 11	Israel Divided	pgs. 96-105
Week 12	Obediah	pgs. 106-114
Week 13	Isaiah	pgs. 115-121
Week 14	Judah After the Fall of Israel	pgs. 122-131
Week 15	Fall of Assyria and Rise of Babylon	pgs. 131-138
Week 16	Ezekiel Prophesies from Exile	pgs. 139-148
Week 17	The Israelite Nation in Exile	pgs. 149-156
Week 18	Daniel's Visions	pgs. 157-166
Week 19	The Story of Esther	pgs. 166-174
Week 20	The Time between the Testaments	pgs. 175-177
Week 21	A New Covenant through Christ: The Beginning of the Gospel Message	pgs. 178-186
Week 22	Jesus's Great Ministry in Galilee	pgs. 186-196
Week 23	Jesus and the Multitudes	pgs. 196-202
Week 24	Jesus's Ministry from Galilee to Judea	pgs. 203-215
Week 25	The Last Supper & Jesus's Crucifixion	pgs. 215-225
Week 26	The Establishment of a New Body of Believers: The Beginning of Christianity	pgs. 226-235
Week 27	Paul's Journeys and Letters	pgs. 236-240
Week 28	Paul's Second Missionary Journey	pgs. 241-246
Week 29	Paul's Third Missionary Journey	pgs. 246-256
Week 30	Paul's Letter to the Romans	pgs. 256-265
Week 31	Paul's Voyage to Rome	pgs. 265-274
Week 32	Paul's Letter to the Philippians	pgs. 274-282
Week 33	Additional Letters Written to Spread the Gospel Message	pgs. 283-291
Week 34	The Letter to the Hebrews	pgs. 292-300
Weeks 35&36	The End of the Journey	pgs. 301-317

Calendar Year Study Schedule (52 weeks)

Week 1	In The Beginning	pgs. 1-8
Week 2	Name Changes	pgs. 8-14
Week 3	Joseph	pgs. 14-20
Week 4	The Passover and the Exodus	pgs. 20-28
Week 5	The Journey through the Desert	pgs. 28-34
Week 6	The Laws of Moses	pgs. 35-41
Week 7	The Israelites' Arrival in Canaan: The Beginning of Life in the Promised Land	pgs. 42-46
Week 8	The Period of the Judges	pgs. 47-52
Week 9	The Story of Ruth	pgs. 53-56
Week 10	The Kings of Israel	pgs. 57-62
Week 11	David and His Psalms	pgs. 62-67
Week 12	King David	pgs. 68-75
Week 13	Psalms for a Troubled Soul	pgs. 75-77
Week 14	King Solomon	pgs. 77-82
Week 15	Solomon's Proverbs	pgs. 83-92
Week 16	Solomon's Song of Songs, & Ecclesiastes	pgs. 93-100
Week 17	Prophets and Prophecies	pgs. 101-105
Week 18	Obadiah	pgs. 106-110
Week 19	Jonah	pgs. 111-118
Week 20	More Prophecies from Isaiah	pgs. 118-126
Week 21	Nahum's Prophecies and King Josiah	pgs. 126-133
Week 22	The First Judeans Exiled	pgs. 133-138
Week 23	Ezekiel Prophesies from Exile	pgs. 139-145
Week 24	Jerusalem Falls	pgs. 146-151
Week 25	Ezekiel's Temple Vision and His Death	pgs. 151-156
Week 26	Daniel's Visions	pgs. 157-161
Week 27	Prophecies of Haggai and Zechariah	pgs. 162-168
Week 28	Malachi's Prophecies	pgs. 169-174
Week 29	The Time between the Testaments	pgs. 175-177
Week 30	A New Covenant through Christ: The Beginning of the Gospel Message	pgs. 178-186
Week 31	Jesus's Great Ministry in Galilee	pgs. 186-193
Week 32	Jesus's Miracles	pgs. 194-200
Week 33	Return to Jerusalem for Feast of Tabernacles	pgs. 201-207
Week 34	Jesus's Final Journey	pgs. 208-215
Week 35	The Last Supper	pgs. 215-221
Week 36	Jesus's Crucifixion	pgs. 221-225

Week 37   The Establishment of a New Body of Believers: pgs. 226-232
            The Beginning of Christianity
Week 38   First Gentile Followers   pgs. 232-238
Week 39   Paul's Letter to the Galatians   pgs. 239-246
Week 40   Paul's Third Missionary Journey   pgs. 246-252
Week 41   Paul's Second Letter to the Corinthians   pgs. 252-256
Week 42   Paul's Letter to the Romans   pgs. 256-262
Week 43   Paul's Arrest and Trial before the Sanhedrin   pgs. 262-267
Week 44   Paul's Letter to the Colossians   pgs. 268-274
Week 45   Paul's Letter to the Philippians   pgs. 274-282
Week 46   Additional Letters Written to Spread the Gospel Message pgs. 283-286
Week 47   Peter's First Letter   pgs. 287-291
Week 48   The Letter to the Hebrews   pgs. 292-297
Week 49   John's First Letter   pgs. 297-300
Weeks 50-52 The End of the Journey   pgs. 301-317

Bibliography

Archaeological Study Bible. NIV version. Grand Rapids: Zondervan, 2005.

Bible Atlas Online by Access Foundation, Edited by Zaine Ridling, accessed May 30, 2016, **https://theologue.wordpress.com/2014/04/30/zaine-ridling-bible-atlas-e-book/**

Bible History Online, accessed October 15, 2015, http://www.bible-history.com/maps.html

Deluxe Then and Now Bible Maps. Torrance: Rose, 2008.

Eerdmans' Handbook to the Bible. Edited by David and Pat Alexander. Grand Rapids: William B. Eerdmans, 1973.

Eusebius' Ecclesiastical History. Translated by C. F. Cruse. Peabody: Hendrickson, 2006.

Glo Bible. NIV version. Orlando: Immersion Digital and Grand Rapids: Zondervan, 2009.

Halley, Henry H. *Halley's Bible Handbook.* 24th ed. Grand Rapids: Zondervan, 1965.

"Jerusalem in the Time of Jesus." *Reader's Digest Atlas of the Bible.* The Reader's Digest Association, Inc. (1981): 184–185.

Josephus. Complete Works. Translated by William Whitson, A. M. Grand Rapids: Kregel, 1978.

Knowing the Bible, accessed October 15, 2015, http://www.knowing thebible.net/tabernacle-1444

Merriam-Webster's Collegiate Dictionary. 11th ed. 2009.

Moore, Mark E. *The Chronological Life of Christ.* Vol. 1 From Glory to Galilee. Joplin: College Press, 1996.

Moore, Mark E. *The Chronological Life of Christ.* Vol. 2 From Galilee to Glory. Joplin: College Press, 1997.

Packer, J. I., Merrill C. Tenney, and William White, Jr. *Nelson's Illustrated Encyclopedia of Bible Facts.* Nashville: Thomas Nelson, 1995.

Rasmussen, Carl G. *Zondervan Atlas of the Bible.* Grand Rapids: Zondervan, 2010.

Reader's Digest Atlas of the Bible. Pleasantville: The Reader's Digest Association, Inc., 1981.

Rose Book of Bible Charts, Maps and Time Lines. Torrance: Rose, 2005.

"Seven Churches of Revelation", accessed October 15, 2015, http://www.biblenews1.com

Strong, James, LL.D., S.T.D. *The New Strong's Expanded Exhaustive Concordance of the Bible.* Red-Letter ed. Nashville: Thomas Nelson, 2001.

Tenney, Merrill C. *New Testament Survey.* Revised by Walter M. Dunnett. Grand Rapids: Wm. B. Eerdmans, 1985.

The Bible Study Site, accessed October 15, 2015, http://www.biblestudy.org/

The Narrated Bible in Chronological Order. Narrated by F. LaGard Smith. NIV version. Eugene: Harvest House, 1984.

The NIV Study Bible, New International Version. Grand Rapids: Zondervan, 1985.

Vine, W. E. *Vine's Expository Dictionary of Old & New Testament Words.* Nashville: Thomas Nelson, 1997.

Wikipedia.org

Zondervan Pictorial Encyclopedia of the Bible. Grand Rapids: Zondervan, 2009.

About the Author

A trained teacher with an advanced degree in Education, Linda has more than 35 years of classroom experience. Over the years, she has developed coursework for a number of classes from the university level to the pre-school stage. In one of her most recent classes, she taught F. LaGard Smith's Daily Bible In Chronological Order, New International Version, Harvest House, 1984. As she prepared this particular class, she was struck by the fact that the Bible, the greatest book ever written, is usually taught topically, jumping from basic Bible stories to the life of Jesus to instruction on Christian principles, and not cover to cover like a regular textbook. Her degree in education, her background in curriculum development and her teaching experience told her no instructor approaches a classroom textbook in this manner. Class always begins at the beginning of the book

where important information establishes a strong foundation of basic concepts and ends at the end of the book where all facts and ideas come together to provide a deeper understanding of the material. Linda decided to use this same approach to help individuals who want to study the Bible from cover to cover. Her Chronological Bible Workbook will direct your study, which begins in Genesis at the beginning of time. As you study, you will travel through events as they occurred. This approach will help you develop a stronger foundation of biblical knowledge leading to a deeper understanding of God's Word. Your study will end in God's Revelation to John at the end of time. Linda believes a cover to cover study of the Bible will allow God to reveal His Word to you in a way like no other

CPSIA information can be obtained
at www.ICGtesting.com
Printed in the USA
BVHW010541290820
587582BV00015B/1115